How to Use This Book

Look for these special features in this book:

SIDEBARS, **CHARTS**, **GRAPHS**, and original **MAPS** expand your understanding of what's being discussed—and also make useful sources for classroom reports.

FAQs answer common **F**requently **A**sked **Q**uestions about people, places, and things.

WOW FACTORS offer "Who knew?" facts to keep you thinking.

TRAVEL GUIDE gives you tips on exploring the state—either in person or right from your chair!

PROJECT ROOM provides fun ideas for school assignments and incredible research projects. Plus, there's a guide to primary sources—what they are and how to cite them.

Please note: All statistics are as up-to-date as possible at the time of publication.

Consultants: Timothy W. (Tyler) Clark, Chief Geologist, North Carolina Geological Survey; Jeffrey J. Crow, Deputy Secretary, North Carolina Office of Archives and History; William Loren Katz

Book production by The Design Lab

Library of Congress Cataloging-in-Publication Data
Heinrichs, Ann.
  North Carolina / by Ann Heinrichs.
     p. cm.—(America the beautiful. Third series)
  Includes bibliographical references and index.
  ISBN-13: 978-0-531-18566-7
  ISBN-10: 0-531-18566-4
  1. North Carolina—Juvenile literature. I. Title.
  F254.3.H449 2008
  975.6—dc21   2007039773

1 2 3 4 5 6 7 8 9 10 R 18 17 16 15 14 13 12 11 10 09

North Carolina

BY ANN HEINRICHS

Third Series

Children's Press®
An Imprint of Scholastic Inc.
New York ★ Toronto ★ London ★ Auckland ★ Sydney
Mexico City ★ New Delhi ★ Hong Kong
Danbury, Connecticut

CONTENTS

OHIO

N W E S

WEST VIRGINIA

KENTUCKY

MARYLAND

D.C.

N.J.

DELAWARE

VIRGINIA

University of North Carolina

North Carolina Museum of Life and Science

WRIGHT

Wright Brothers National Memorial

Grandfather Mountain

Blue Ridge Parkway

International Civil Rights Center and Museum

Mount Mitchell State Park

Roanoke

Albemarle Sound

TENNESSEE

Appalachian Mountains

WINSTON-SALEM

GREENSBORO

DURHAM

North Carolina State Capitol

Tar

World's Largest Chest of Drawers

RALEIGH

North Carolina State Fair

ASHEVILLE

NORTH CAROLINA

North Carolina Apple Festival

CHARLOTTE

Pee Dee

Neuse

Pamlico Sound

Outer Banks

Cape Hatteras National Seashore

Afro-American Cultural Center

National Hollerin' Contest

Cape Fear

WILMINGTON

SOUTH CAROLINA

USS North Carolina Battleship Memorial

GEORGIA

0   50
Miles

ATLANTIC OCEAN

QUICK FACTS

State capital: Raleigh
Largest city: Charlotte
Total area: 53,819 square miles
   (139,391 sq km)
Highest point: Mount Mitchell, 6,684
   feet (2,037 m) in Yancey
Lowest point: Sea level along the
   Atlantic coast

Welcome to North Carolina!

HOW DID NORTH CAROLINA GET ITS NAME?

In 1629, King Charles I of England granted a large parcel of land to Sir Robert Heath. Today's North and South Carolina were both within its boundaries. King Charles named this land the Province of Carolana, after himself. (*Carolana* comes from *Carolus*, the Latin word for "Charles.") The province was later renamed Carolina. It eventually split into North Carolina and South Carolina, and they are neighboring states today.

NORTH CAROLINA

8

READ ABOUT

Hanging Rock
at Hanging Rock
State Park

CHAPTER ONE

LAND

★

NORTH CAROLINA IS A PLACE OF VARIED LANDSCAPES. Its mountains are among the tallest and most rugged east of the Mississippi River, and its coastal plains are low and flat. High in the western mountains rises Mount Mitchell. At 6,684 feet (2,037 meters), it's the state's highest point. Hundreds of miles to the east, the land drops down to sea level along the Atlantic coast. Within an area of 53,819 square miles (139,391 square kilometers), the state's climate ranges from oppressively hot to bitterly cold. North Carolina's plants and animals are as diverse as its environment.

Figure Eight Island is near Wrightsville Beach on the Atlantic Ocean.

WHERE IS NORTH CAROLINA?

North Carolina is in the southeastern United States, in the middle of the country's Atlantic coast. The state measures about 505 miles (813 km) from east to west and about 190 miles (306 km) from north to south. North Carolina borders Virginia to the north, Tennessee to the west, and South Carolina to the south. A small section of North Carolina's southwestern edge borders Georgia. And the Atlantic Ocean stretches along the state's eastern border.

LAND REGIONS

North Carolina has three major land regions. From west to east, they are the Mountain Region, the Piedmont, and the Atlantic Coastal Plain.

The Mountain Region

In the far western part of the state, North Carolina's Mountain Region covers about 10 percent of the state's total area. The mountains there are the southern section of the great Appalachian Mountain range, which runs along the eastern United States. Many of these forest-covered mountains rise more than 1 mile (1.6 km) high. In the valleys, rich soil makes for fertile farmland.

The major mountains in this region are the Blue Ridge Mountains and the Great Smoky Mountains. Others include the Black Mountains, the Brushy Mountains, the Pisgah

ELISHA MITCHELL: MEASURING THE MOUNTAIN

Elisha Mitchell (1793–1857) was a geologist who taught at the University of North Carolina at Chapel Hill. He measured a certain peak in the Blue Ridge and declared it the highest peak in the eastern United States. When a colleague challenged him, Mitchell went back to measure again. During that trip, a thunderstorm struck. Mitchell slipped off a cliff over a waterfall and drowned. The peak, Mount Mitchell, was named for him, and he is buried on the summit.

? Want to know more? See http://docsouth.unc.edu/browse/bios/pn0001194_bio.html

Sunset over the Pisgah National Forest, seen from the Blue Ridge Parkway

North Carolina Topography

Use the color-coded elevation chart to see on the map North Carolina's high points (dark red to orange) and low points (green to dark green). Elevation is measured as the distance above or below sea level.

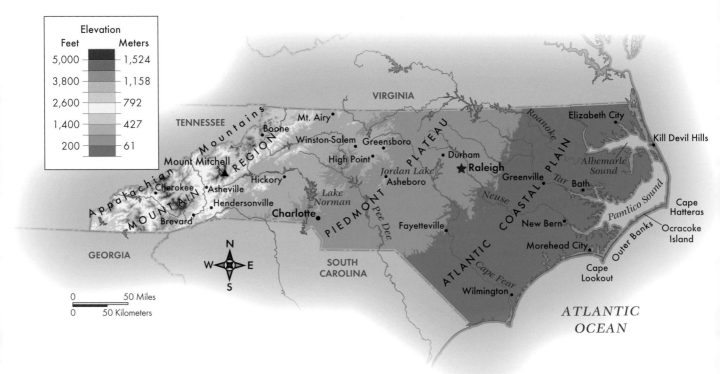

Mountains, and the Great Balsam Mountains. Gases released from trees create a bluish-gray haze over the Blue Ridge Mountains, whose peaks form much of the border between Tennessee and North Carolina.

The Black Mountains are part of the Blue Ridge range. They are the highest mountains in the eastern United States. Among them rises Mount Mitchell, North Carolina's highest peak.

The Great Smoky Mountains—sometimes called the Smokies—are named for the smokelike haze that

North Carolina Geo-Facts

Along with the state's geographical highlights, this chart ranks North Carolina's land, water, and total area compared to all other states.

Total area; rank . . . . . 53,819 square miles (139,391 sq km); 28th
Land area; rank . . . . . 48,711 square miles (126,161 sq km); 29th
Water area; rank . . . . . . 5,108 square miles (13,230 sq km); 10th
Inland water; rank . . . . . . 3,960 square miles (10,256 sq km); 6th
Territorial water; rank . . . 1,148 square miles (2,973 sq km); 10th
Geographic center . . . . Chatham County, 10 miles (16 km)
northwest of Sanford
Latitude . . . . 34° N to 36°21' N
Longitude . . . . 75°30' W to 84°15' W
Highest point . . . . Mount Mitchell, 6,684 feet (2,037 m),
in Yancey
Lowest point . . . . Sea level along the Atlantic coast
Largest city . . . . Charlotte
Longest river . . . . Cape Fear River, 200 miles (322 km)

Source: U.S. Census Bureau

WOW Twelve North Carolinas could fit inside Alaska, the largest state. And Rhode Island, the smallest state, would fit inside North Carolina almost 35 times!

blankets their high valleys and peaks. Considered part of the Blue Ridge Mountains, the Smokies straddle part of the border between North Carolina and Tennessee.

The Piedmont

The Piedmont is North Carolina's central region, covering about 45 percent of the state. It's named for the Piedmont Plateau, a part of the eastern United States that lies between the Appalachian Mountains and the Coastal Plain. Rolling hills and low mountains cover the Piedmont, with the highest elevations in the west and

A hiker enjoys the view of Whitewater Falls in Nantahala National Forest.

the lowest in the east. Piedmont mountains include the Uwharrie Mountains, the Sauratown Mountains, Pilot Mountain, and the Brushy Mountains, an offshoot of the Blue Ridge.

Many rivers and streams cut valleys through the Piedmont as they rush from the western mountains toward the coast. At the eastern edge of the Piedmont, called the Fall Line, rivers cascade down in waterfalls and rapids toward the low-lying Coastal Plain.

The Atlantic Coastal Plain

The Atlantic Coastal Plain covers eastern North Carolina. The Sandhills in the southwest coastal plain divide this region from the Piedmont. The coastal plain is a lowland that slopes gently toward the sea. Like the Piedmont, the Atlantic Coastal Plain makes up about 45 percent of the state's total land area.

Millions of years ago, the ocean covered what is now the coastal plain. Water that did not completely drain from the land gathered in swampy areas. The Great Dismal Swamp of northeastern North Carolina, extending into Virginia, is one of the largest swamps in the country.

The northeastern part of North Carolina's coastal plain is called the **Tidewater** region. The Tidewater has many marshes, lakes, and sand dunes, and most of the state's wetlands. Farther inland, where the land is drier, the sandy soil is ideal for agriculture. Over the years, as tidewaters rose and fell along the coast, they cut deeply into the land, creating broad **sounds** and wide river mouths. As a result, the coast is jagged and irregular.

ISLANDS, CAPES, AND SHIPWRECKS

Dozens of islands lie off the coast of North Carolina. The largest islands are long, narrow sandbars called barrier islands. These sandy islands protect the mainland from the full force of ocean waves. The outermost barrier islands are a chain called the Outer Banks, which encloses Albemarle Sound in the north and Pamlico Sound in the south. The major islands of the Outer Banks are Bodie, Roanoke, Hatteras, and Ocracoke.

At the end of some barrier islands, narrow points called capes jut out into the ocean. Beyond the capes, the land continues out to sea slightly under the surface of the water. These sandy or rocky stretches are called shoals. Over the years, countless ships have run aground in the shallow waters of these shoals.

The most notorious capes are Cape Hatteras, Cape Lookout, and Cape Fear. Diamond Shoals, just beyond Cape Hatteras, is the site of hundreds of shipwrecks.

WORDS TO KNOW

tidewater *low coastal land that is affected by tides*

sounds *long, wide inlets of the ocean along a coast*

Scallop shells

In the 1700s, Ocracoke was known as a hideout for the pirate Edward Teach, better known as Blackbeard.

Cape Hatteras Lighthouse at Cape Hatteras National Seashore

In fact, the entire coastline of the Outer Banks is called the Graveyard of the Atlantic. Its treacherous waters, along with strong ocean currents and stormy weather, have sunk thousands of ships and cost an untold number of lives.

In the 1800s, North Carolina began to build lighthouses at points along the Outer Banks. A lighthouse was first built on Cape Hatteras in 1803. Cape Hatteras Lighthouse, with its distinct candy-striped exterior, is the tallest lighthouse in North America. Lighthouses also stand on Bodie and Ocracoke islands, Cape Lookout, and many other points along the coast.

CLIMATE AND WEATHER

Along the coastal plain, the waters of the Atlantic Ocean prevent summer and winter temperatures from getting too extreme. In that area, winter temperatures seldom drop below 40 degrees Fahrenheit (4 degrees Celsius), and the summer highs average lower than 89°F (32°C). Although coastal temperatures are mild, fierce storms often hit the coast. Thick fog drifts in from the sea, too, making it hard for sailors and boaters to see.

The western mountains are the coldest part of the state. Summertime in the mountains is cool, and winters can be bitterly cold. In July, the average temperature in the mountains is a pleasant 65°F (18°C), while January averages about 28°F (–2°C). The state's lowest recorded temperature was set on Mount Mitchell on January 21, 1985, when it reached a bone-chilling –34°F (–37°C).

The Piedmont gets hotter summers than the coast and milder winters than the mountains. In fact, most of North Carolina's recorded temperatures above 100°F (38°C) have occurred in the Piedmont. Fayetteville registered the state's highest recorded temperature on August 21, 1983, when it reached 110°F (43°C).

Weather Report

TEMPERATURE **110°F**   TEMPERATURE **–34°F**

This chart shows record temperatures (high and low) for the state, as well as average temperatures (July and January) and average annual precipitation.

Record high temperature . . . . .110°F (43°C) at Fayetteville
on August 21, 1983
Record low temperature . . . . . . –34°F (–37°C) at Mount Mitchell
on January 21, 1985
Average July temperature . . . . .79°F (26°C)
Average January temperature . . . . .40°F (4°C)
Average annual precipitation . . . . .43 inches (109 cm)

Source: National Climatic Data Center, NESDIS, NOAA, U.S. Dept. of Commerce

WEATHER EXTREMES

Hurricanes hit the North Carolina coast every few years. Only Florida and Louisiana get more hurricanes than North Carolina. In 1999, Hurricane Floyd hit the state, producing extensive flooding. The storm resulted in 35 deaths in North Carolina and caused billions of dollars in damage.

Thunderstorms drench the state an average of 50 days a year. They often come with high winds and hail that damage trees and houses. Tornadoes are most frequent on the coastal plain. A series of 25 tornadoes in 1984 killed 40 people. Sleet and freezing rain are common in the Piedmont. They coat tree limbs and power lines with ice, sometimes causing them to break and fall.

Blizzards, or fierce snowstorms, can sweep through the mountain regions. The Blizzard of 1993 dumped more than 50 inches (127 centimeters) of snow on Mount Mitchell in just three days. The town of Boone, in northwestern North Carolina, endured winds up to 110 miles (177 km) an hour.

Red-bellied turtles sunning on a log in a North Carolina lake

WORD TO KNOW

precipitation *all water that falls to the earth, including rain, sleet, hail, snow, dew, fog, or mist*

Most of North Carolina's **precipitation** comes in the form of rain. The mountains get the most precipitation, followed by the coastal plain. Snowfall is heaviest in the mountains, which get about 40 inches (100 cm) of snow a year. People on the coastal plain get little or no snow in the winter.

ANIMAL LIFE

Wander through the woods on a summer night, and you're bound to hear a high-pitched whistling sound. It's a spring peeper, one of North Carolina's many frogs. This little tree frog's "peep" is a sure sign that spring has come. Some of the state's frogs live in trees. Others inhabit the wetlands of the Piedmont and the Coastal Plain. Common reptiles are turtles, lizards, and snakes, including poisonous ones such as copperheads, rattlesnakes, and water moccasins. North Carolina is also home to alligators, which live along the swampy southeastern coast.

BANKER PONIES

Ocracoke Island, on the Outer Banks, is home to a colony of wild horses called banker ponies. They're not really ponies, but small horses with a stocky build. The origin of the banker ponies is shrouded in mystery. Some say they are descended from wild horses that swam or washed ashore from shipwrecked Spanish ships centuries ago.

Today, the Ocracoke herd numbers 25 to 30 horses. The National Park Service tends to them in a large, fenced pasture. Another herd lives around Corolla on Bodie Island. Attempts to fence them in have not been successful. More than 100 wild horses live on the island of Shackleford Banks, where they roam free.

Banker pony

White-tailed deer can be found all over the state. Black bears live mainly in the western mountains and the Coastal Plain. Small populations of bobcats, mountain lions, elk, wild boars, and wolves roam the mountains, too. Other animals of the woodlands and fields include rabbits, foxes, squirrels, opossums, raccoons, coyotes, and mice.

Cardinals, mockingbirds, Carolina wrens, bluebirds, and warblers are common songbirds in North Carolina. Wild turkeys, grouse, quail, partridges, woodcocks, and doves live in many parts of the state. Several species of ducks, geese, and swans spend their winters near the coast. Other shorebirds are gulls, egrets, terns, pelicans, cranes, ospreys, and plovers.

A great egret in the marsh at Pea Island National Wildlife Refuge

There are 24 species of lungless salamanders in Great Smoky Mountains National Park. They breathe through the walls of tiny blood vessels in their skin and the linings of their mouths and throats.

Land was cleared to make way for this housing development in Hendersonville.

ENDANGERED SPECIES

Many kinds of animals are endangered in North Carolina. Wood storks, roseate terns, and red-cockaded woodpeckers are endangered birds. Leatherback, hawksbill, and Atlantic Kemp's ridley sea turtles are also endangered. Endangered mammals include the eastern cougar and the Carolina northern flying squirrel. The Virginia big-eared bat and several other bat species are endangered. Among the state's many conservation projects is the Red Wolf Recovery Plan. This program is reintroducing endangered red wolves into the wild in the northeastern part of the state.

Eastern cougar

The rivers and streams are home to freshwater fish such as bass, catfish, crappie, perch, shad, and trout. Off the Atlantic coast, some of the saltwater species are tuna, bluefish, marlin, sailfish, swordfish, mackerel, red snapper, and shark. Shellfish such as oysters, clams, and mussels are found in the coastal waters. Crayfish, smaller relatives of lobsters, live around rivers and streams.

More than 70 animal species in North Carolina are becoming scarce. Hunting and trapping has cut down some animal populations. Others are disappearing through loss of their natural habitats as people clear land and drain wetlands for development.

PLANT LIFE

North Carolina has a wide diversity in its plant life. That's because the state has such a variety of elevations and climate zones, as well as abundant rainfall. Almost every tree species that is found east of the Rocky Mountains grows in North Carolina. Oak trees are especially diverse. Black, white, scarlet, turkey, pin, post, and live oak are just some of the state's oak species.

Forests once covered almost all of North Carolina. But much of that forestland was cut or burned to make way for farms. Today, about 60 percent of the state is forested. The heaviest growth is in mountainous areas and parts of the Coastal Plain. Because temperatures are cooler in the western mountains, the trees there are species common to more northerly regions. There you'll find hemlock, fir, spruce, maple, and birch trees. The Piedmont has a mixture of pines and hardwoods such as oak, hickory, and poplar. Pine trees are the major species on the Coastal Plain. The blooms of dogwoods, redbuds, azaleas, rhododendrons, and mountain laurels brighten the forests.

Trees that tolerate a lot of water are found in the swampy areas and near rivers. They include cypresses, Atlantic white cedars, and gum trees. Palmettos, members of the palm tree family, grow along the southern coast. The southeastern swamps are home to a rare insect-eating plant called the Venus flytrap. It traps insects using bristles that grow on the surface of its leaves. When an insect brushes against the bristles, the trap snaps shut.

Rhododendron blossoms

North Carolina National Park Areas

This map shows some of North Carolina's national parks, monuments, preserves, and other areas protected by the National Park Service.

	National Park area
NB	National Battlefield
NHS	National Historic Site
NHT	National Historic Trail
NMEM	National Memorial
NMP	National Military Park
NP	National Park
NS	National Seashore
NST	National Scenic Trail
PKWY	Parkway

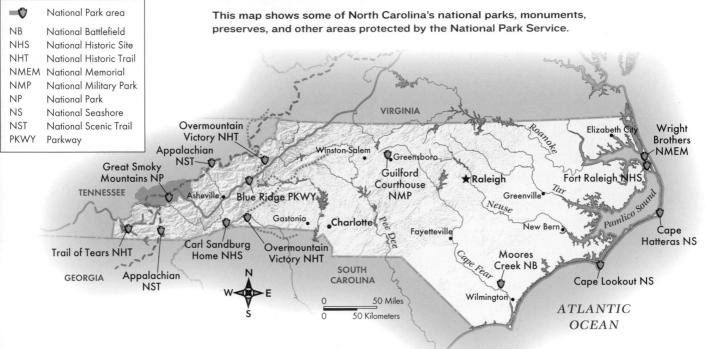

HEALING HERBS

The mountains of North Carolina are home to many herbs that are used for medicinal, or healing, purposes. Native Americans knew them well and passed on their knowledge to early European settlers. Goldenseal is used to combat infections and to help kill tumors. Black cohosh has been used to decrease swelling and increase blood circulation. Native Americans used bloodroot to treat fevers. Today, it's used to treat skin cancer and skin growths such as warts. Bloodroot is also used in toothpaste and mouthwash to reduce plaque and gingivitis, a gum disease. Scientists are researching its effects on brain tumors, too.

Bloodroot

Pine trees have a special place in the state's history. In the 1700s and 1800s, North Carolina had a thriving business in naval stores, which are pine-based products used in shipbuilding. They were made from the sticky resin that oozes from cuts in the tree. Naval stores such as tar, pitch, and turpentine were valuable as water repellents, sealers, and preservatives.

PRESERVING THE ENVIRONMENT

North Carolinians want to keep their land, air, and water healthy and clean. Hazardous wastes, which pollute the environment with toxic chemicals, have been drastically reduced since the mid-1990s. The state government monitors the quality of the state's air and works to reduce smoke, haze, harmful vehicle and industry **emissions**, and even farm animal odors. It tests and regulates the water in rivers, lakes, and streams, as well as underground water sources and wastewater. These are just a few of the measures North Carolina takes to preserve its natural resources for generations to come.

WORD TO KNOW

emissions *substances released into the air*

These trees in the Smoky Mountains show the damaging effects of acid rain, which is caused by chemical emissions.

SEE IT HERE!

HOLMES EDUCATIONAL STATE FOREST

This forest is in the Blue Ridge Mountains near Hendersonville. Signs along the trails describe how forests are managed, how trees are thinned, and how fires can help and hurt the forest. The Talking Tree Trail features trees with a recorded message describing themselves, their history, and their surroundings. Like all forests, this one provides food and cover for animals. While visiting, you may see white-tailed deer, foxes, gray squirrels, cottontail rabbits, skunks, opossums, ruffled grouse, or wild turkeys.

READ ABOUT

Early hunters
used spears to
kill mastodons
and other big
game animals.

c. 10,000 BCE

Paleo-Indians begin to inhabit what is now North Carolina

c. 8000 BCE

North Carolina's Archaic culture begins

▲ c. 1000 BCE

People of the Woodland culture begin settling in villages

CHAPTER TWO

FIRST PEOPLE

★

B ETWEEN 10,000 AND 8000 BCE, THE ICE AGE WAS DRAWING TO A CLOSE. Mastodons and bison roamed the land. Early people called Paleo-Indians hunted these massive animals, as well as smaller animals. They also gathered wild plants. Paleo-Indians moved from place to place as the food supplies changed. In time, the climate became warmer, creating a different environment, and people adapted to the changes.

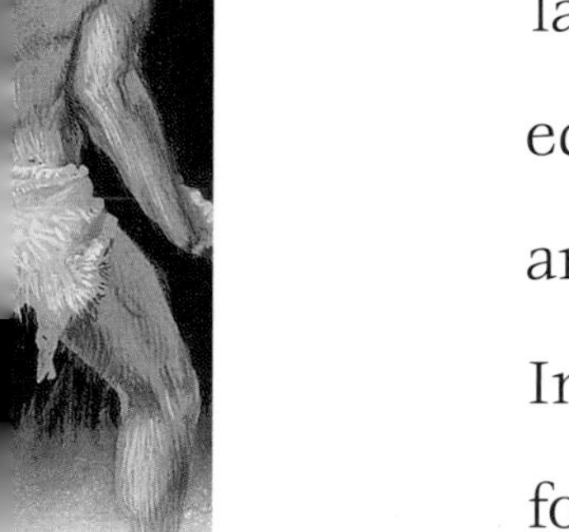

◄ **c. 1000** CE

The Mississippian culture begins, marked by extensive farming

c. 1000–1400

The Pee Dee culture thrives in the southern Piedmont

1540

Europeans and North Carolina's Native Americans make contact

Mississippian artifact

Spear points from the Woodland culture

ARCHAIC PEOPLES

As the large animals became extinct, or died out, people turned to hunting small animals and gathering fruits, roots, nuts, and berries. They also caught fish and collected shellfish. This period lasted from about 8000 to 1000 BCE. By this time, North Carolina's climate, animals, and plants were much as they are today.

Like their Paleo-Indian ancestors, the Archaic people lived in temporary settlements. As time went on, they began making grinding tools, bowls, and clay vessels. For hunting, they developed a spear-throwing device called the atlatl. Some also planted small gardens and grew gourd squashes. They used the gourds as cups, spoons, and dippers.

Some Archaic people left traces of their way of life in drawings carved into stone, called petroglyphs. A large boulder called Judaculla Rock in western North Carolina depicts turtles, lizards, humans holding hands, and many mysterious shapes. No one knows why these figures were carved or what they mean.

Judaculla Rock is named after a slant-eyed giant in Cherokee legend. As it leaped from a nearby mountain, it is said to have left its seven-toed footprint in the rock!

THE WOODLAND AND MISSISSIPPIAN CULTURES

Starting in about 1000 BCE, people began to settle in villages, usually along rivers. Known as Woodland peoples, they hunted and gathered wild foods and also practiced extensive agriculture. They grew wild plants in their farm plots, as well as crops such as squash, sunflowers, corn, beans, and tobacco.

Around 1000 CE, people in some parts of what is now North Carolina began to build larger villages, some surrounded by **palisades**, or fences made of wooden stakes. Agriculture became a major activity, and people planted fields of corn and other crops. This is called the Mississippian culture.

The Mississippian peoples also introduced new ways to make pottery, build towns, and govern. Mississippian groups banded together in chiefdoms under strong leaders. Some built flat-topped, pyramid-shaped mounds of earth as bases. On top of these mounds, they built wooden temples and houses for chiefs.

THE PEE DEE CULTURE

Only small bits of evidence remain to tell us how people lived during the Mississippian period. But one group of people in the southern Piedmont left behind a wealth of **artifacts**. They lived in the Pee Dee River valley from about 1000 to 1400 CE, and they are called the Pee Dee people.

A shell gorget (a piece of armor) from the Mississippian culture

WORDS TO KNOW

palisades *fences of logs set vertically into the ground close to each other to create a protected village*

artifacts *objects remaining from a particular period of time*

A large earthen mound stands at the Pee Dees' Town Creek site. At one time, a temple stood atop the mound. It faced a large plaza where the Pee Dee people held public meetings and ceremonies. Several structures stood along the edge of the plaza, including a burial house and homes for chiefs, priests, and other high-ranking officials. A palisade encircled all these buildings. Villagers lived outside the town center, where they grew corn.

Pee Dee people carried on much trade with other groups. They obtained copper from the Great Lakes region and seashells from the coast. They made the shells into beads, necklaces, and pins. With the copper, they fashioned rattles, ear ornaments, pendants, and axes.

SEE IT HERE!

TOWN CREEK INDIAN MOUND

Much of the Pee Dees' ceremonial site has been reconstructed as the Town Creek Indian Mound historic site near Mount Gilead. Here you can see the temple atop the great mound and a burial house. A palisade encloses the site, just as it did hundreds of years ago. At the visitor center, exhibits feature tools, pottery, jewelry, and other objects from the site. The nearby learning center offers demonstrations of Native American skills and crafts.

Huts and longhouses protected by a palisade, near present-day Hyde County

Native American Peoples

(Before European Contact)

This map shows the general area of Native American peoples before European settlers arrived.

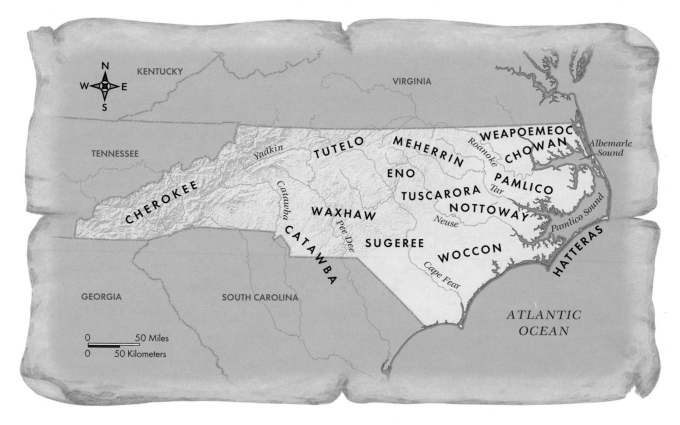

PEOPLES OF THE COASTAL PLAIN

North Carolina's coastal peoples caught great quantities of herring, sturgeon, mullet, and other fish. They also gathered crabs, oysters, clams, scallops, and mussels. Corn was their major crop, but they also raised pumpkins, squash, sunflowers, and beans. In the coastal forests and marshes, they hunted bears, deer, rabbits, squirrels, and waterbirds. They collected edible roots, nuts, and seeds and gathered wild strawberries, mulberries, grapes, and other fruits. They ate foods raw, dried, or cooked in clay pots.

Farther inland on the Coastal Plain lived the Tuscarora, Meherrin, and Nottoway peoples. Instead of having chiefs who ruled a wide area, each village governed itself. The people traded with their coastal neighbors for pottery, shells, and jewelry. They cultivated some of North Carolina's richest farmland. Men tilled fields of corn and beans, and they hunted deer, bears, raccoons, and rabbits.

CHEROKEE ANCESTORS

From about 1000 to 1450, the Pisgah culture flourished in the western mountains and river valleys. Pisgah people lived in villages surrounded by wooden walls. They built rectangular homes in a circle around a central plaza. They wove wooden posts together with branches and packed them with clay to build walls. Pisgahs made roofs of bark or woven plant materials. Larger villages included flat-topped earthen mounds with buildings on top that were probably used for religious ceremonies.

Villagers grew corn as well as beans and squash. Pisgah people also hunted deer and bears. They ate the meat, made the skin into clothing and bags, and used the bones as tools. They also ate smaller animals and caught fish. In the fall, they gathered nuts such as acorns and hickory nuts. Fruits and berries rounded out their diet.

The Qualla culture arose around 1400. The Qualla way of life was very much like that of the Pisgah people, except that Quallas built rounded mounds with a large, round town house, or council house, on top. Several hundred people could gather inside the town house for important meetings and religious ceremonies. They kept a sacred fire burning in the house at all times.

Another group came to call the Qualla people *Cherokee,* meaning "people with another language." Some Cherokees called themselves the "people of Kituhwa." This ancient town near today's Bryson City in western North Carolina is believed to be the first Cherokee town. A sacred fire burned in Kituhwa for centuries.

CHEROKEE CULTURE

Cherokees were organized into seven clans, or groups, each with a special role or skill. Members wore different colors of feathers to indicate their clan. Each clan governed itself, with adults gathering in the council house to discuss important issues. Each clan had a peace chief, a war chief, and a priest.

Cherokee society was matrilineal—that is, people traced their kinship through the mother's side of the family. Cherokee women were in charge of gardening, as well as preparing food and taking care of the family and its property. Women wore wraparound skirts and poncho-like blouses. They planted and harvested corn, beans, squash, and sunflowers and gathered wild plants. In stone ovens, they cooked foods such as cornbread, soups, and stews.

A wooden mask used in the Cherokee snake dance

Picture Yourself . . .

at a Cherokee New Green Corn Festival

Today is a big day, and you are up at dawn. A messenger has visited your clan and collected a barely ripened ear of corn from your fields, announcing that the New Green Corn Festival is beginning. You greet the new day with prayers. You walk to the riverbank with your family and other clan members and wade into the water. Then you pray to the seven directions—north, south, east, and west, as well as the sky above, the earth below, and the center, where you are. Later, at the festival, there are ceremonies, dances, and stickball games. Kernels of corn from each of the seven Cherokee clans are offered in the sacred fire. Then food is prepared for everyone from the new corn. After the festival, you and your family eat the new corn.

WORD TO KNOW

blowguns *weapons that consist of tubes through which darts are blown*

Cherokee basket

Cherokee men were in charge of hunting, fishing, fighting wars, and making peace. They shaved their heads and wore leggings and a breechcloth—a cloth anchored at the waist that hung down in the front and back. The men decorated their faces and bodies with paint and tattoos. Both men and women wore deer-skin moccasins on their feet. Men hunted deer, wild turkeys, and other animals with bows and arrows and **blowguns**. They fished with spears, fishing poles, and nets. For river transportation, they made dugout canoes from logs.

Boys went hunting and fishing with their fathers, and girls cultivated the fields and took care of the home with their mothers. Children had a chance to play, too. One popular game involved throwing a dart through a rolling hoop. Children also played with cornhusk dolls and other toys. Teenagers and men played a stickball game similar to lacrosse.

Cherokee homes were made of river cane, a tall bamboo plant that grew by the riversides. The people sealed the cracks between the reeds with a clay-based plaster and made roofs of bark or woven grasses. Cherokees also used river cane to weave baskets and fishnets and to make blowguns and flutes. Other crafts included pottery made from baked clay, cups made from squash gourds, and ceremonial pipes carved from stone.

Cherokees held six main festivals throughout the year. Special dances accompanied each one. The Spring New Moon Festival in March celebrated the renewal of life and the new planting season. The New

Green Corn Festival, or Busk, took place in July or August, when the corn was beginning to ripen. It celebrated the emergence of new corn and marked the new year. The Ripe Corn Festival in late September gave thanks for the harvested corn. The Great New Moon Festival in October celebrated the creation of the world, which Cherokees believed took place at this time. Ten days later was the Friendship Festival, in which individuals pledged respect and friendship to one another. Last, the Bouncing Bush Festival was a joyous ceremony thanking the Great Spirit for his many blessings.

Native American ceremonial dance

A WAY OF LIFE ENDS

Europeans began exploring North and South America in the late 1400s. It was not long before they reached North Carolina. The first to arrive was Giovanni da Verrazano, an Italian sailing for the French. He reached North Carolina's coast and explored the Cape Fear area in 1524. Hernando de Soto of Spain was the next to arrive. Traveling overland from present-day Mexico, he reached southwestern North Carolina in 1539. Once Europeans and Native Americans made contact, life for American Indians began to change.

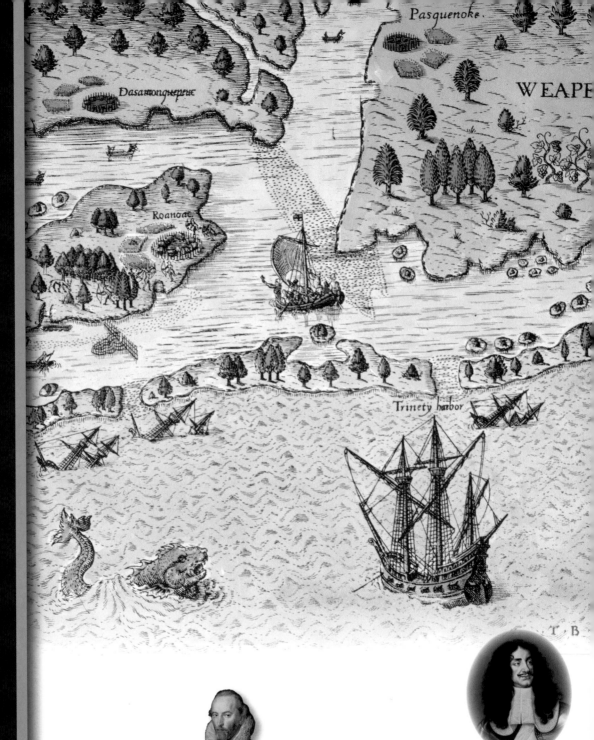

34

READ ABOUT

The arrival of
English settlers at
Roanoke Island

1585 ▶

Sir Walter Raleigh
sends settlers
to establish an
English colony on
Roanoke Island

1590

Members of a new
colony on Roanoke
Island disappear;
their settlement is
called the Lost Colony

1663 ▲

King Charles II grants
the Carolina colony to
eight lords, who divide
it into three counties

CHAPTER THREE

EXPLORATION AND SETTLEMENT

★

NEITHER FRANCE NOR SPAIN WAS INTERESTED IN MAKING SETTLEMENTS NEAR PRESENT-DAY NORTH CAROLINA. It was the English who first came to stay. Sir Walter Raleigh hoped to establish a colony in North America as a base where English ships could stop for repairs and supplies. If it succeeded, it would be the first English colony in North America.

1711

Fighting breaks out between Tuscaroras and white settlers in the Tuscarora War

1781

Colonial and British forces clash in the Battle of Guilford Courthouse

1789 ►

North Carolina becomes the 12th state of the United States of America

European Exploration of North Carolina

The colored arrows on this map show the routes taken by explorers between 1524 and 1539.

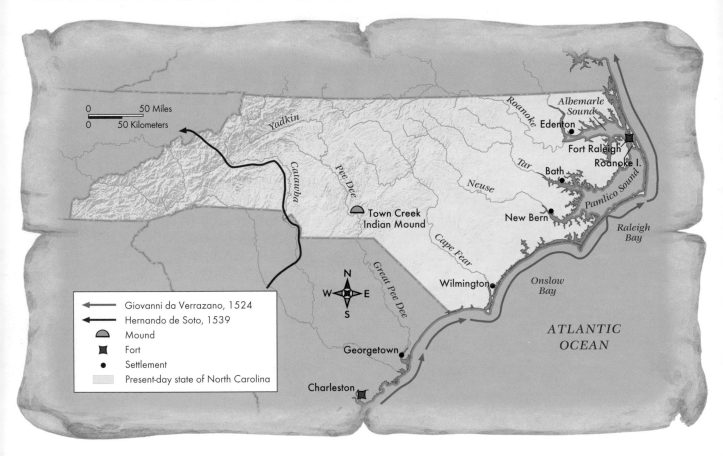

THE LOST COLONY

On July 13, 1584, an English ship landed on Roanoke Island, along the coast of what is now North Carolina. The Englishmen were impressed by its abundant natural resources and the welcome they received from Native Americans. Two Indians returned with them to England, where the explorers made a very favorable report.

In 1585, Raleigh sent a shipload of 108 men across the Atlantic Ocean, and they settled on Roanoke Island. Contrary to the explorers' report, food was not natu-

rally abundant on the island. In fact, the Indians were skilled farmers who carefully cultivated what land they could. Life was hard for the European settlers, and they went back home the next year.

Raleigh again sent colonists across the sea—this time, more than 100 men, women, and children. One of the colonists, John White, would be their governor. White had high hopes for the colony. Among the colonists were his daughter and son-in-law. In 1587, the colonists settled into their new home on Roanoke Island. Four weeks later, White's daughter gave birth to a baby girl—Virginia Dare. She was the first English baby born in North America.

Needing more supplies, White soon sailed back to England, leaving the colonists behind. When he returned in 1590, White faced a shocking scene. The colony had been deserted; everyone was gone.

The only clue to the disappearance was the word *CROATOAN* carved on a wooden post. The Croatans, or Hatteras, were a group of Native Americans who lived on a nearby island, but they had been friendly toward the English colonists. This colony came to be called the Lost Colony. Over the years, people have come up with many theories about the Lost Colony, but no one knows what really happened to it.

Governor White and other Englishmen discovering the abandoned Roanoke Colony

FAQ

Q8 HOW MANY PEOPLE WERE IN THE LOST COLONY?

A8 There were 91 men, 17 women, and 9 children—a total of 117 people. The 118th colonist, Virginia Dare, was born after her parents arrived.

Charles II of England

THE PROVINCE OF CAROLINA

Many years passed before England attempted another colony in North Carolina. In 1629, the English king, Charles I, granted a strip of land to Sir Robert Heath. It included today's North and South Carolina, and it was named the Province of Carolana, after the king. (*Carolana* comes from *Carolus*, the Latin word for "Charles.") Heath never set up a colony there.

Meanwhile, just to the north, English people were settling in the Virginia Colony. Around 1653, some Virginia colonists moved south and settled in the Albemarle Sound area. They became North Carolina's first permanent European settlers.

Eventually, King Charles's son, Charles II, made a new land grant. In 1663, he changed Carolana to Carolina and granted it to eight of his loyal noblemen. He declared them the lords proprietors, or landlords, of the Province of Carolina. Four of the lords proprietors were slave traders. They encouraged new settlers to use enslaved Africans on their lands, which extended south through today's Georgia and into northern Florida. The initial labor force in the colonies was indentured whites, who were bound to work for a set period of time to pay off a debt and were freed after that time. Gradually enslaved Africans, who were forced to work for their entire lifetime, became the laborers in the colonies.

The proprietors divided their province into three counties. Albemarle County was in the north, and Clarendon County was in the Cape Fear area. Craven County was in today's South Carolina.

Governing the province was difficult. Colonists resented the taxes their leaders were collecting for tobacco exports. In 1677, John Culpepper led a revolt called Culpepper's Rebellion. Colonists threw out their governor and ruled themselves for more than a year. The province's government continued to struggle to control the entire region. By 1712, North and South Carolina had split apart, with each having a separate governor.

SETTLERS AND THE TUSCARORA WAR

Meanwhile, many new settlers were coming to North Carolina. Some were seeking religious freedom, such as French Protestants called Huguenots and people of the Quaker faith from England. Others simply hoped to make a fresh start farming or trading in a new land. They came from Germany, Switzerland, Ireland, and other countries, as well as from neighboring colonies.

Settlements spread south along the coast from Albemarle Sound. Many Huguenots settled between Albemarle and the Pamlico River, and the riverside town of Bath was founded in 1705. It was North Carolina's first permanent European town. Farther south, alongside the Neuse River, Swiss and German immigrants established New Bern in 1710. They named it after the city of Bern, Switzerland.

These and other settlers were taking over more and more Tuscarora land. In addition, British traders had been kidnapping Tuscarora men, women, and

Picture Yourself . . .

on a Colonial Farm
Your family moved deep into the wilderness to live far from the colonial government in the East. Here in the pine forest, your closest neighbors live miles away. When you arrived, you and your brothers helped your father clear the brush and build a home out of pine logs. Your mother and sisters covered the windows with oil paper. They stuffed straw mattresses and sewed cozy quilts for the beds.

It's springtime, and your father is turning the soil with his ox-drawn plow. You follow behind, placing grains of corn in the furrows. At night, everyone eats the pheasant and rabbits your brothers hunted in the woods. There are shiny berries, too, plucked from the underbrush. Then it's time to gather around the fireplace for reading aloud. At last, by candlelight, you make your way to bed.

Many North Carolinians tolerated Blackbeard because they could buy cheap stolen goods from him.

Blackbeard

children to sell as slaves. Smallpox and other European diseases had wiped out much of the Tuscarora population, too. These upheavals threw Native culture into disarray. By 1711, Tuscarora frustrations boiled over, and they began attacking settlers. Troops from both North and South Carolina joined the fight, and hundreds of people were killed on both sides in what came to be called the Tuscarora War. Defeated by 1715, most Tuscaroras left the area.

BLACKBEARD THE PIRATE

Piracy was another problem facing the struggling colony. Pirates lurked among the sandbars and inlets of the Outer Banks, attacking merchant ships and robbing their cargoes of guns, liquor, and other goods. The most notorious pirate of them all was Edward Teach, better known as Blackbeard.

Blackbeard was a fearsome figure with his bristling beard and colorful coat, two swords at his waist, and bands of pistols and knives across his chest. From aboard his ship, *Queen Anne's Revenge*, he commanded more than 300 pirates and seized more than 40 ships. In 1718, he was killed at his Ocracoke Inlet hideout in a bloody battle with the British Royal Navy.

THE ROYAL COLONY

Great Britain bought North Carolina from the proprietors in 1729. North Carolina became a royal British colony, with governors appointed by the king. New

A REFUGE IN THE SWAMP

During the era of slavery, the Great Dismal Swamp between North Carolina and Virginia became a refuge for untold numbers of escaped former slaves and indentured laborers, as well as some Native Americans who had been forced off their land. Some families in the Dismal Swamp lived in small towns, while others lived in smaller villages or family groups. For decades, authorities were afraid to send in troops to these well-armed and determined societies to try to recapture the former slaves and laborers. They knew people would fight to the death for their liberty rather than face returning to servitude. It is a mystery who led these settlements or how they resisted conquest. But their presence was a thorn in the side to the slave system—and stood as a shining hope for those still in chains.

Bern was the colonial capital, and the colony had a two-house legislature, or lawmaking body.

By this time, North Carolina was home to about 36,000 people. Most lived in the coastal area, where wealthy planters raised tobacco and rice on large plantations worked by enslaved people from Africa. Farther west, in the Piedmont region, were mainly small-scale family farms. Tensions often simmered between these two regions. Eastern lawmakers charged taxes on the westerners' land and seized their farms if they couldn't pay.

In 1768, frustrated farmers formed the Regulator movement to

WILLIAM TRYON: GOVERNOR WITH A PALACE

William Tryon (1729–1788) was the royal governor of the Province of North Carolina from 1765 to 1771. He built such a magnificent mansion in New Bern that it came to be called Tryon's Palace. The building is considered North Carolina's first capitol. Tryon and other wealthy leaders and tax collectors provoked poor farmers to organize the Regulator movement. After Tryon crushed the Regulators, he went on to be governor of New York. Tryon's Palace is now a state historic site.

? **Want to know more?** See www.tryonpalace.org/palace.html

Regulator farmers battling British troops in the 1770s

WORD TO KNOW

WORD TO KNOW

Parliament *the legislature in Great Britain*

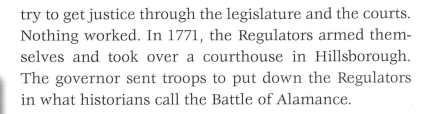

Q8 WHAT WAS THE STAMP ACT?

A8 According to the 1765 Stamp Act, American colonists had to pay a tax on all printed papers, including legal documents, newspapers and publications, and even playing cards!

MINI-BIO

PENELOPE BARKER: HOSTESS OF THE EDENTON TEA PARTY

Penelope Barker (1728–1796) was one of the wealthiest women in North Carolina. On October 25, 1774, she invited 50 prominent Edenton women to a tea party. In reality, she was organizing a protest against the British tea tax. "We women have taken too long to let our voices be heard," she told her guests. They agreed and signed a statement swearing never to buy British tea again. Throughout the colonies, women followed Barker's example.

? Want to know more? See www. northcarolinahistory.org/commentary/20/entry/

try to get justice through the legislature and the courts. Nothing worked. In 1771, the Regulators armed themselves and took over a courthouse in Hillsborough. The governor sent troops to put down the Regulators in what historians call the Battle of Alamance.

THE REVOLUTIONARY WAR

By 1733, there were 13 British colonies along the coast. Colonists were growing angry because they had no representatives in the British **Parliament**, yet they had to pay taxes on goods shipped from Great Britain. The 1765 Stamp Act and other tax laws provoked protests throughout the colonies. In 1773, in the Massachusetts Colony, people dumped a shipment of British tea overboard into Boston Harbor to protest the tea tax. North Carolinians staged their own "tea party" in 1774. Penelope Barker got 50 women in Edenton to sign a paper swearing they would no longer drink British tea or buy British cloth.

Angry representatives from North Carolina and the other colonies met in Philadelphia, Pennsylvania, in 1774. They formed the First Continental Congress to discuss their opposition to Great Britain's unfair laws. In April 1775, the conflicts boiled over into the Revolutionary War (1775–1783). Some North Carolinians were still loyal to Britain, but others wanted independence. Armies from both

The colonists and British troops clash at the Battle of Guilford Courthouse in 1781.

sides clashed in the Battle of Moore's Creek Bridge on February 27, 1776. North Carolina's first Revolutionary War battle ended in defeat for the pro-British forces.

Two months later, on April 12, North Carolina representatives met in Halifax. They issued the Halifax Resolves, affirming that North Carolina wanted independence from Great Britain. North Carolina was the first colony to make that decision. All 13 colonies then approved the Declaration of Independence, announcing it to the public on July 4.

The major Revolutionary War battle on North Carolina soil was the Battle of Guilford Courthouse. On

AFRICAN AMERICAN SOLDIERS

By the time of the Revolutionary War, 75,000 North Carolinians were enslaved. During the war, General George Washington commanded a North Carolina brigade of 68 African Americans. More than 5,000 other African Americans served in the Continental army and navy.

WORDS TO KNOW

constitution *a written document that contains all the governing principles of a state or country*

Bill of Rights *the first ten amendments to the Constitution, which list the fundamental rights guaranteed to Americans*

March 15, 1781, American general Nathanael Greene led colonial forces against British general Charles Cornwallis. With their freedom at stake, the colonists fought fiercely. Cornwallis said, "I never saw such fighting since God made me. The Americans fought like demons." Although the British won this battle, it severely weakened Cornwallis's forces and was a turning point in the war. Just a few months later, Cornwallis surrendered at Yorktown, Virginia. This essentially ended the fighting, and the war formally ended in 1783 with the signing of the Treaty of Paris.

BECOMING A STATE

The colonies had become the United States of America when they declared their independence in 1776. Soon after, they had adopted a system of governance outlined in the Articles of Confederation, the country's first **constitution**. Government under the Articles emphasized strong self-governing states. After the formal end of the Revolutionary War, representatives from each state met again in Philadelphia in 1787. This time, they formed the Constitutional Convention and drew up a constitution that included a strong central, or federal, government for the new country. Each state would have to ratify, or approve, the constitution to gain official statehood.

In 1788, North Carolinians met at the Hillsborough Convention to discuss the constitution, which they rejected. They thought it gave the national government too much power and left people without important rights. After the **Bill of Rights** was added to the Constitution, North Carolinians agreed to ratify it. On November 21, 1789, North Carolina became the 12th state to join the Union.

North Carolina: From Territory to Statehood
(1663–1789)

This map shows the original North Carolina territory and the area (in yellow) that became the state of North Carolina in 1789.

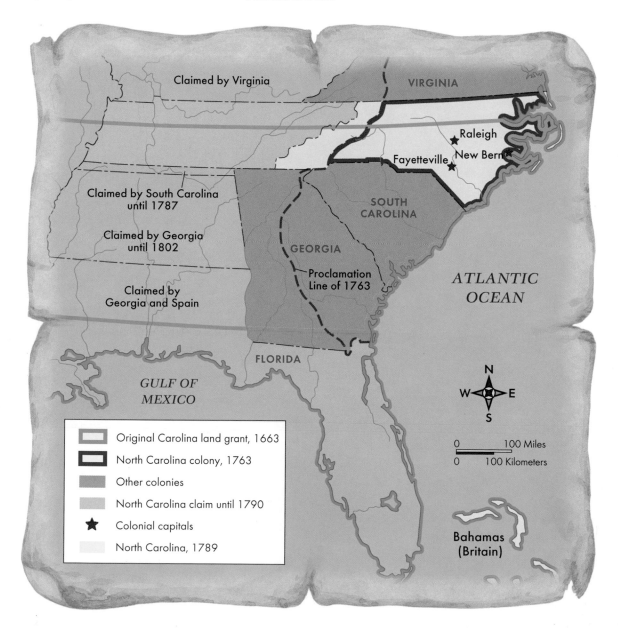

Claimed by Virginia

VIRGINIA

Raleigh

Fayetteville   New Bern

Claimed by South Carolina
until 1787

SOUTH
CAROLINA

Claimed by Georgia
until 1802

GEORGIA

Proclamation
Line of 1763

ATLANTIC
OCEAN

Claimed by
Georgia and Spain

FLORIDA

N
W   E
S

GULF OF
MEXICO

0   100 Miles
0   100 Kilometers

Original Carolina land grant, 1663

North Carolina colony, 1763

Other colonies

North Carolina claim until 1790

★ Colonial capitals

North Carolina, 1789

Bahamas
(Britain)

READ ABOUT

A North Carolina
family and their
log cabin

1835

*North Carolina revises
its constitution, giving
more power to the
western counties*

▲1838

*The U.S. government
forces the Cherokee
people to move to
Oklahoma along the
Trail of Tears*

1861

*North Carolina secedes
from the Union after
the Civil War begins*

CHAPTER FOUR

GROWTH AND CHANGE

★

AFTER THE REVOLUTIONARY WAR, NORTH CAROLINA CONTINUED TO RELY ON AGRICULTURE. It did not undergo the rapid industrial growth that northern states experienced at the time. To some people, North Carolina seemed to be asleep. It was called the Rip Van Winkle State, after the storybook character who slept for 20 years.

1868
North Carolina rejoins
the Union

1900
*New provisions in the
state constitution deny
most African Americans
the right to vote*

1903 ►
*Near Kitty Hawk, the
Wright brothers make the
first successful powered
airplane flight*

48

MILTON FURNITURE MAKER

Thomas Day (c. 1801–1861) was an African American cabinetmaker and maker of fine furniture. He started his business in Milton in the 1820s. In 1848, he moved his shop into Milton's Old Union Tavern building. There he operated the largest furniture-making business in North Carolina, employing as many as 80 workers. Besides making furniture, Day crafted mantelpieces, staircases, window and door frames, and other decorative woodwork. Collectors and museums prize his fine furniture today.

Enslaved workers plant rice on a North Carolina plantation.

FARMS AND INDUSTRIES

In 1790, North Carolina had a population of almost 394,000. Only Virginia and Pennsylvania had more residents. At that time, about 100,000 of North Carolina's people were African Americans. Most were enslaved workers on large plantations growing corn, wheat, cotton, or tobacco. Slaves were supervised by overseers, who were paid according to the amount of crops the workers produced. Typically, slaves worked 14-hour days in the summer and 10-hour days in the winter, with Sundays off. Children were sent into the fields to work by age nine or ten. Some slaves planned revolts, but little is known about them. Uprisings were quickly crushed, and news about them was suppressed.

Rice flourished in the marshy coastal lands. But planters didn't know how to cultivate it. They paid high prices for slaves from West Africa's so-called Rice Coast. Its climate was much like that of the Cape Fear region, along North Carolina's southeast coast. Highly

skilled Africans planted, harvested, and processed the American rice. They also brought their cooking traditions and developed a **dialect** that blended English and African languages. Their unique way of life, called Gullah culture, has almost died out in North Carolina, although it survives in South Carolina and Georgia.

Not everyone in the state lived by farming. North Carolinians were developing many small industries to serve their local communities. Gristmills ground grain into flour, and cotton gins separated cotton seeds from the fibers. Sawmills cut logs into lumber, and paper mills turned wood products into paper. Iron forges turned out tools, kettles, nails, and wagon wheel rims. Furniture making was a growing industry, too. The state's first cotton textile (cloth) mill opened in 1815. Shipbuilding was an important industry on the coast, along with naval stores such as turpentine. Some enslaved men and women became skilled mechanics, nurses, cooks, servants, jockeys, midwives, carpenters, blacksmiths, coachmen, stonemasons, and plantation managers.

Gold mining was another North Carolina industry. It began in 1799, when 12-year-old Conrad Reed went fishing in Little Meadow Creek near Midland. He saw a 17-pound (7.7 kilogram) rock glistening in the creek and brought it home. Conrad's family used the rock as a doorstop for three years. Then a jeweler recognized it as gold and bought it for $3.50. This was the first verified gold find in the United States. Soon the nation's first gold rush was on, as gold mines sprang up throughout the region. In 1837, the Charlotte Mint was established for making gold coins.

WORD TO KNOW

dialect *a version of a language*

North Carolina was the nation's top gold-producing state from the early 1800s until the California gold rush began in 1849!

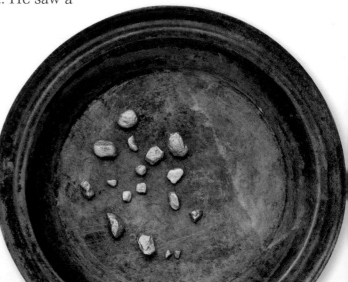

Mining pan with gold nuggets

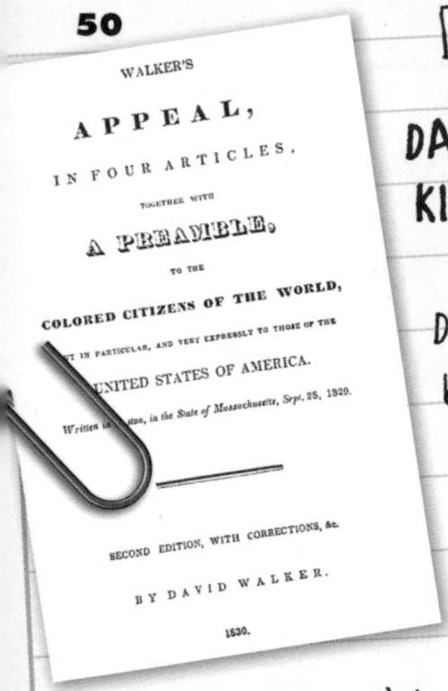

WALKER'S

APPEAL,

IN FOUR ARTICLES.

TOGETHER WITH

A PREAMBLE,

TO THE

COLORED CITIZENS OF THE WORLD,

BUT IN PARTICULAR, AND VERY EXPRESSLY TO THOSE OF THE

UNITED STATES OF AMERICA.

Written in Boston, in the State of Massachusetts, Sept. 28, 1829.

SECOND EDITION, WITH CORRECTIONS, &c.

BY DAVID WALKER.

1830.

DAVID WALKER: KILL OR BE KILLED

David Walker (1785–1830) was born in Wilmington as a free black. Eventually, he moved to Boston, Massachusetts, where he opened a used-clothing store. He also wrote many articles for the African American newspaper *Freedom's Journal*. In 1829, Walker published a pamphlet called *Walker's Appeal* (shown above), urging African Americans to rise up against their oppressors and "kill or be killed." Plantation owners tried to suppress it and even put a price on Walker's head. One day, he was found dead on his doorstep.

? **Want to know more?** See www.massmoments.com/moment.cfm?mid=188

WORD TO KNOW

abolitionists *people who work to end slavery*

CONSTITUTIONAL REFORMS AND ABOLITIONISTS

People in the Piedmont and farther west had been frustrated since at least the middle of the 18th century by easterners' control of the state government. In 1835, the state held a constitutional convention in Raleigh. It introduced sweeping reforms. Now voters, instead of the legislature, would elect the governor, and each county could elect at least one member to the legislature's house of representatives. To hold public office, a person could now be Christian, rather than specifically Protestant, which allowed Roman Catholics to be officeholders.

These and other reforms had far-reaching effects. The number of voters increased, and westerners had a strong voice in their government. A system to fund schools was established, and roads and railroads were built. Manufacturing began to expand. At last, North Carolina could shed its Rip Van Winkle reputation.

Some changes to the constitution took away rights, though. In 1776, North Carolina had granted voting rights to "free persons of color" who owned property. The 1835 reforms took that right away. Native Americans and free blacks who had been voting could no longer vote. This restriction was made out of concern that the slave system was being weakened by the influence of a growing number of **abolitionists** and by slave uprisings.

Meanwhile, several abolitionist societies were active in the state. The Quaker religious group was especially devoted to the cause. By the 1820s, North Carolina Quakers had launched a strong campaign to aid African Americans. They raised $5,000 to help 350 freed slaves resettle in Free States. A North Carolina Quaker couple, Levi and Catherine Coffin, helped thousands of slaves escape on the Underground Railroad, a network of safe houses that hid runaway slaves on their way to freedom in the North.

THE TRAIL OF TEARS

When Europeans began to arrive in what is now North Carolina, Native American life began to change. At first, the Indians welcomed the new-comers. They introduced the settlers to new crops and wild plants and taught them new ways to hunt, cultivate, and prepare foods. They

MINI-BIO

LEVI COFFIN: PRESIDENT OF THE UNDERGROUND RAILROAD

When Levi Coffin (1798–1877) was growing up in New Garden, North Carolina, he saw a group of enslaved people passing by in chains. They told him they had been taken away from their families and were chained to keep them from going back. This awakened young Levi's sympathy for enslaved people. Later, in Indiana and Ohio, he and his wife helped thousands of slaves escape to freedom. He became known as the President of the Underground Railroad.

? **Want to know more?** See www.indianahistory.org/pop_hist/people/coffin.html

The Trail of Tears, painted by Robert Ottokar Lindneux

MINI-BIO

SEQUOYAH: "TALKING LEAVES" FOR THE CHEROKEE PEOPLE

Sequoyah (c. 1770–1843) was born in the village of Taskigi in western North Carolina (now in Tennessee). His Cherokee mother belonged to the Paint Clan, and his father was a white trader. Sequoyah was fascinated by white people's documents, calling them "talking leaves." By 1821, he had developed a writing system for the Cherokee language. Each of its symbols represents a syllable. Soon thousands of Cherokees could read and write their own language, and Cherokee-language newspapers and books began to be published.

 Want to know more? See www.georgia encyclopedia.org/nge/Article.jsp?id=h-618&hl=y

CHEROKEE HERO

Tsali (?–1838) was a Cherokee who had a farm near Bryson City. In 1838, U.S. troops rounded up his family to relocate them. Tsali and his brother-in-law overpowered the soldiers, and one was accidentally shot. Tsali and his family escaped into the Great Smoky Mountains, where hundreds of other Cherokees were hiding. But Tsali was found and executed. According to Cherokee legend, he agreed to give his life in exchange for the lives of the other **fugitive** Cherokees.

WORD TO KNOW

fugitive *a person who tries to flee or escape*

shared their knowledge of medicinal herbs and other healing practices. Over the course of 300 years, however, settlers became more and more greedy for Indian lands.

To make way for white farms and industry, President Andrew Jackson signed the Indian Removal Act in 1830. It called for the relocation of all Native Americans who lived east of the Mississippi River to Indian Territory, where Oklahoma is now. Jackson expected the Indians to move voluntarily, but they did not want to leave. In 1838, the U.S. government forced the Cherokee people to move from their homeland in a long march called the Trail of Tears.

In North Carolina, the U.S. Army rounded up Cherokees at gunpoint and sent them into camps. The roundup was so swift that many didn't even have time to gather their belongings. Some had to go without foot coverings or shoes. From the camps, they were forced to walk 1,200 miles (2,000 km) to Indian Territory.

Over mountains and rivers they were marched, some carrying others. Thousands died along the way. Cherokees call this tragic march *Nunna daul Isunyi*—"the trail where we cried," or the Trail of Tears. Several hundred Cherokees refused to be removed, and

The Battle of New Bern, March 14, 1862

their descendants survive in North Carolina today. They form the Eastern Band of Cherokee Indians and have a reservation in western North Carolina.

THE CIVIL WAR

By the 1860s, enslaved Africans made up about one-third of North Carolina's total population. The country as a whole was deeply divided over the issue of slavery. Northern states wanted to end slavery's expansion, but Southern planters wanted slave labor to keep their plantations running. As the slavery dispute heated up, South Carolina seceded, or withdrew, from the Union in 1860. Other Southern states followed, forming the Confederate States of America. The Confederacy prepared for war, and in April 1861—when Confederate troops fired on Fort Sumter in the harbor at Charleston, South Carolina—the Civil War began.

North Carolinians weren't eager to secede. They tried to work out compromises and preserve the nation

This poster was used to recruit African Americans to fight for the Union army.

as long as they could. Finally, they realized they could not fight against their fellow slaveholders. In May 1861, North Carolina seceded and joined the Confederacy. Though tens of thousands of North Carolinians fought for the Confederacy, many had been forced into service and the desertion rate was high. North Carolinians were in several ways divided by the Civil War. Many farmers with small holdings didn't see the fight to retain slavery as their own fight but that of the plantation owners.

Some North Carolinians—including more than 5,000 black men—served in the Union army. Many African Americans saw the war as their opportunity for freedom. In 1864, a Virginia paper reported that 500 to 600 black runaways in North Carolina's Currituck and Camden counties were raiding plantations and disrupting Confederate operations. The Lowry band—a mix of

Confederate soldiers crossing the Pee Dee River, 1865

whites, African Americans, and members of the Lumbee Indian Nation—also fought the Confederacy. After they were arrested and forced to help the Confederate cause, the Lowry band fled to launch attacks inside the Confederacy.

Ordinary white North Carolinians were divided in their response to the war. Some did all they could to help the troops. Ministers donated church bells to be melted down and made into cannons. Women ripped down curtains and took up their carpets to make uniforms, bedding, and tents. Textile mills made reams of cloth, but it wasn't enough. Women who hadn't touched spinning wheels in years sat down to spin cotton yarn. Others did all they could to end the war, such as protesting the draft, the right of the Confederate troops to seize property, and taxes imposed to support the war.

FAQ

Q8 BEFORE THE CIVIL WAR, WERE ALL AFRICAN AMERICANS IN NORTH CAROLINA ENSLAVED?

A8 No. African Americans were more likely to be free of slavery in North Carolina than in many other Southern states. In 1860, more than 30,000 African Americans in North Carolina were free blacks. Another 300,000 people in the state were enslaved.

FAQ ★ ★ ★

Q: HOW MANY NORTH CAROLINIANS FOUGHT AND DIED FOR THE CONFEDERACY?

A: About 125,000 North Carolinians signed up to fight for the Confederacy. More than 40,000 were killed in action or died from disease during the war.

SEE IT HERE!

BENTONVILLE BATTLEFIELD

Exhibits at the Bentonville Battlefield Visitor Center in Four Oaks help bring the Civil War to life with battle sounds and a recorded narration. Just press a button to see all the major battlefield maneuvers unfold before your eyes. Red and blue lights represent the Union and Confederate armies. Nearby, you can tour the Harper family home, which Union troops took over to serve as a field hospital for wounded soldiers. Historical markers along area roads describe events of the three-day battle.

Although most of the fighting raged in other states, 20 battles were fought on North Carolina soil. In 1864, Union general William T. Sherman and his troops had marched through Georgia, burning and destroying everything in their path. Next they moved through the Carolinas. As Sherman's forces made their way through the state, thousands of enslaved men, women, and children left plantations to follow them to freedom. When black Union troops liberated Wilmington in 1865, one soldier wrote, "Men and women, old and young, were running through the streets. We could truly see what we had been fighting for." Another said, "I could do nothing but cry to look at the [people] so overjoyed."

The bloodiest of the North Carolina conflicts was the Battle of Bentonville, which took place March 19–21, 1865. Confederate general Joseph Johnston was ordered to "concentrate all available forces and drive back Sherman." Johnston and his soldiers were worn out, but they put up a fight until they had to surrender. The Civil War ended in April 1865. About one-sixth of all the Confederate war dead were North Carolinians.

RECONSTRUCTION

After the war came a difficult period called Reconstruction. Federal troops occupied the former Confederate states and enforced many reforms. In 1868, North Carolina changed its constitution to give African Americans their freedom and African American men the right to vote.

This illustration shows children outside a school run by the Freedman's Bureau, 1868

A group of former slaves and some 20 percent of white North Carolinians formed an **alliance** that was responsible for drafting and passing the 1868 constitution. After this, North Carolina was allowed to rejoin the Union.

The new constitution asserted the right of children to a public school education. Former slaves had insisted that the constitution include a provision for public schools. They considered the right to an education an essential part of their new freedom, as well as a way for them to protect it. Most schools for former slave children were opened by **missionary** societies and the U.S. government's Bureau of Refugees, Freedmen, and Abandoned Lands, commonly called the Freedman's Bureau. In 1869, a white missionary teacher in Fayetteville wrote, "The colored people came from far and near to attend the 'Dedication' of the first schoolhouse built for colored children in this county. The whites are a little jealous, as it surpasses all of theirs. . . . Three of my scholars [teachers] leave this month to take charge of country schools. . . . We now have a hundred and seventy scholars and constantly increasing."

WORDS TO KNOW

alliance *an association between groups that benefits all the members*

missionary *related to trying to convert others to a religion*

By 1870, black officials had been elected to local offices, and John Hyman, a former slave, was elected to the U.S. Congress. All did not go smoothly, though. Former planters and their allies formed the Ku Klux Klan (KKK), a racist organization that terrorized African American officeholders and voters. Klansmen threatened, beat, and even killed to keep African Americans and their white supporters from voting.

White judges and juries would not convict the Klansmen for these crimes. Governor William Holden denounced the Klan activities, but he was **impeached** and removed from office for abusing his position in an attempt to oppose Klan violence. Congress's effort at Reconstruction and equal justice lasted only three years in North Carolina.

Many former slaves found themselves still laboring on farms. Plantation owners divided their farms into smaller portions called tenant farms. Tenant farmers, or sharecroppers, rented the land, paying their rent with crops. White landowners often cheated them and refused to let them leave.

INDUSTRIAL GROWTH AND RACIAL TENSIONS

North Carolina's textile and furniture industries grew quickly after the war. Dozens of textile mills dotted the Piedmont, turning out cotton and woolen yarn and cloth. The industry grew from 85 textile mills in 1870 to 177 mills in 1899. Furniture making grew from small, local shops to large-scale manufacturing plants in the 1880s. By 1900, 44 furniture factories were operating in High Point, Mebane, Greensboro, and nearby towns. Many of these factories were built alongside railroad tracks so the furniture could be shipped out easily.

WORD TO KNOW

impeached *charged with official misconduct while in office*

A North Carolina tobacco market, 1800s

Tobacco was another growing industry. The state had 111 tobacco factories in 1870. Many prepared chewing tobacco, in high demand at the time, but cigars were growing in popularity, too. In the 1880s, machines that made cigarettes were introduced. Durham and Winston-Salem became big centers for processing tobacco.

African Americans worked mainly in the tobacco industry, and some became business owners themselves. In eastern North Carolina, more than a dozen African Americans were elected to the state legislature between 1868 and 1889, and three African Americans were elected to the U.S. House of Representatives. One was George Henry White of Tarboro, who had once been enslaved. White had educated himself, secured a law degree, and served six years in the state legislature and eight years as a government attorney. Black and white voters in his district elected him to Congress twice. White told his fellow congressmen they would have to solve the problems of racial injustice: "You have got this problem to settle. I speak this in all charity, I speak this with no hos-

George Henry White

tility." White was the last former slave to sit in the House of Representatives and the last black man to serve in Congress for decades.

Some whites, however, were threatened by African Americans' increasing economic and political power in the late 1890s, and there was a resurgence in white violence toward blacks. Several hundred white men in Wilmington burned the offices of the black-owned *Wilmington Daily Record* newspaper in 1898. After the riot, whites forced black officials out of office and took over the city government. In 1900, changes in the state constitution made it almost impossible for blacks to vote or hold office.

For the next 60 years, African Americans were **segregated** from white Americans. They could not go to the same schools or eat in the same restaurants. Because many white businesses refused to serve blacks, many African Americans opened businesses that served other African Americans. The North Carolina Mutual Life Insurance Company, founded in 1898 in Durham, grew to be the largest single African American corporation in the country. It provided low-cost insurance to thousands of black families in many states besides North Carolina, proving that people of color could run a successful business when given a chance. However, North Carolina and other southern states did not offer nonwhite residents much chance for a decent education or a good job.

WORD TO KNOW

segregated *separated from others, according to race, class, ethnic group, religion, or other factors*

A segregated café in Durham

INNOVATIONS AND WAR

In 1900, two inventive brothers traveled from Ohio to Kitty Hawk, on the Outer Banks. Orville and Wilbur Wright were experimenting with flying machines, and Kitty Hawk had just the right winds and soft sand they needed. On December 17, 1903, after three years of test flights, they piloted their *Wright Flyer* for about 200 feet (60 m). The Wright brothers had built the first successful airplane!

Another modern invention, the automobile, was arriving on the scene, too. In 1909, North Carolina began issuing its first motor vehicle driver's licenses. A state highway commission was set up in 1915 to build and maintain roads throughout the state. Eventually, North Carolina would be known as the Good Roads State.

Activities such as road building were put on hold during World War I (1914–1918). When the United States entered the war in 1917, Wilmington shipbuilders began making warships. Farmers stepped up their production of food crops, cotton, and tobacco to supply the troops. Textile workers made uniforms, blankets, socks, and tents. Other factory workers turned out ammunition, wagon wheels, and airplane propellers. Men and women of all races volunteered for military service. United in a common cause, they helped bring about victory.

Wilbur Wright watches his brother, Orville, pilot the *Wright Flyer* at Kitty Hawk on December 17, 1903.

READ ABOUT

Boys operating
cotton-thread
spooling
machines in
Cherryville, 1908

1930s

*North Carolinians
suffer through the
Great Depression*

1959

*Research Triangle Park
opens, beginning an era
of high-tech growth*

▲1960

*Four black students in
Greensboro hold the
nation's first sit-in to
protest racial segregation*

MORE MODERN TIMES

★

B Y THE 1920s, NORTH CAROLINA WAS THE NATION'S TOP PRODUCER OF TEXTILES, FURNITURE, AND TOBACCO. But these industries came to a near screeching halt in 1929, when the country plunged into a period of economic hard times called the Great Depression. Millions of people lost their jobs, businesses, and farms.

1972 ▶

Governor James Holshouser Jr.
and U.S. senator Jesse Helms
(above) become the first North
Carolina Republicans elected to
those offices since the 1890s

1980s

The textile and
furniture industries
begin to decline

2007

The business magazine
Forbes names North
Carolina as the best
place to do business or
start a career

Civilian Conservation Corps workers filling a gully on eroded farmland in Yanceyville, 1940

THE GREAT DEPRESSION

In 1932, Franklin D. Roosevelt was elected president. He soon put into effect a series of programs that he called the New Deal. The New Deal programs helped provide jobs and other relief. One important program in North Carolina was the Agricultural Adjustment Administration (AAA), which paid farmers to grow less tobacco and other crops. This helped improve prices for crops, which had dropped dramatically during the Depression. Another New Deal program, the Civilian Conservation Corps (CCC), provided jobs for thousands of young men in North Carolina parks and forests. They built roads, planted trees, and worked on many other projects.

WAR AND POSTWAR PROSPERITY

North Carolina's economy bounced back during World War II (1939–1945). As in World War I, North Carolinians contributed to the war effort. More than 360,000 North

Carolina men and women of all races served in the armed forces. The state had more than 20 military camps, training posts, military hospitals, and supply centers.

Many women went to work in industrial plants. They helped make war supplies such as uniforms, parachutes, ammunition, ships, and aircraft and radar parts. No other state produced more clothing for the troops. More than three-fourths of all the mica used in gas masks and other goods came from North Carolina mines. Farmers helped feed the U.S. troops with corn, wheat, soybeans, potatoes, chickens, and hogs.

After the war, the logging industry boomed as people moved into suburbs and built new homes. The textile and furniture industries also grew, since people needed furniture, upholstery, and draperies for their new homes. Tourism flourished, too. People who had served on North Carolina military bases had seen the state's beauty. Many came back to vacation in the mountains and coastal areas or to drive the Blue Ridge Parkway. This scenic mountain route, which began as a New Deal project, was completed after the war. It connects the Shenandoah National Park in Virginia with the Great Smoky Mountains National Park in Tennessee and North Carolina.

THE CIVIL RIGHTS MOVEMENT

During the 1950s, African Americans began to accelerate their demand for the same **civil rights** as white Americans. In response, the Ku Klux Klan became more violent. In Monroe, Klansmen drove through black neighborhoods firing guns to intimidate parents and children who tried to **integrate** local swimming pools or schools.

Robert Williams, a local leader of the National Association for the Advancement of Colored People (NAACP),

WOW

Early in World War II, German submarines were attacking American merchant ships, often along the coast of North Carolina. Navy warships were sent in to stop the attacks. More ships and submarines were sunk in North Carolina's waters than anywhere else in North America!

WORDS TO KNOW

civil rights *basic human rights that all citizens in a society are entitled to, such as the right to vote*

integrate *to bring together all members of society*

tried to handle matters peacefully by appealing to city council members for help. They did nothing. Then he appealed to state and federal officials to protect the rights of African Americans, and again nothing was done. Finally, Williams called on African Americans to arm themselves. The next time armed Klansmen attacked an African American neighborhood, black North Carolinians fired back. After that, Williams recalled, "The Klan didn't have any more stomach for this type of fight. They stopped raiding our community."

The Lumbees, a group with mixed African and Native American heritage, also challenged the KKK. As Klansmen prepared to light a huge cross, 500 armed Lumbees charged at them, firing their guns in the air and yelling. The Klansmen fled.

Many authorities date the peaceful beginnings of the modern civil rights movement to February 1, 1960, when four black freshmen at North Carolina Agricultural and Technical College in Greensboro sat down at a "whites only" Woolworth's lunch counter, ordered coffee, and refused to leave when they were not served. Three of the young men had grown up in Greensboro and had shopped in the store before, but they had never sat at its lunch counter. One of the students, David Richmond, later admitted "all of us

Members of the Ku Klux Klan dressed in white robes and hoods, and they often burned crosses as a way of threatening African Americans and other citizens.

Four young men during the second day of the protest at the Woolworth's lunch counter in Greensboro, 1960

were afraid" because they knew they could be arrested or face violence, but "we went ahead and did it." Another student, Franklin McClain, later described his feelings: "I felt as though I had gained my manhood, so to speak, and not only gained it, but had developed quite a lot of respect for it."

The store manager closed the store, but the students' simple act of peaceful protest impressed other students, including whites, and spread to other cities across the country. Women at Bennett College, a black school, joined the campaign, and two days later white women at Greensboro's Women's College of the University of North Carolina took part. In a few weeks, the Woolworth's in Greensboro had 80 protesting students of both races. **Sit-ins** spread to Durham, Char-

WORD TO KNOW

sit-ins *acts of protest that involve sitting in seats or on the floor of an establishment and refusing to leave*

SEE IT HERE!

GREENSBORO HISTORICAL MUSEUM

You'll get a close-up feel for the civil rights movement at the Greensboro Historical Museum. It displays four chairs from the original Woolworth's counter where the Greensboro Four staged their sit-in. Other exhibits feature information on the four protesters and timelines of the sit-in and the civil rights movement. You'll also see newspaper headlines about the sit-in—an event that surprised the nation and changed the course of American history.

MINI-BIO

JOSEPH McNEIL: ONE OF THE FOUR

Joseph McNeil (1942–) moved with his family from Wilmington to New York after he graduated from high school, but McNeil went back to North Carolina to attend college in Greensboro. Returning to college after a winter vacation, he was refused food service in the Greensboro bus station. He then resolved to protest segregation, and he and three friends staged the Greensboro sit-in. McNeil later worked as a stockbroker and a banker and became a major general in the Air Force Reserves.

? Want to know more? See www.pbs.org/independentlens/februaryone/four.html

lotte, Winston-Salem, and Chapel Hill. Outside, protesters marched with picket signs supporting the sit-ins. A Chapel Hill student carried a sign reading, "We . . . picket to protest the lack of dignity and respect shown us as human beings." People demonstrated through kneel-ins at churches, wade-ins at swimming pools, and bowl-ins at bowling alleys. A youth movement was taking over the battle for civil rights.

Another milestone for civil rights also began in North Carolina in the spring of 1960. That year, 200 students and others met at Shaw University, a black university in Raleigh founded for former slaves soon after the Civil War, to form the Student Nonviolent Coordinating Committee (SNCC). Ella Baker, a Shaw graduate, proposed the organization. She and other women promoted the idea of direct action to secure equal rights to attend schools and colleges, use libraries, and vote. Baker said, "The younger generation is challenging you and me" and "asking us to forget our laziness and doubt and fear, and follow our dedication to the truth to the bitter end." SNCC also welcomed white people who were willing to fight racial injustice. This movement born

Ella Baker of the Student Nonviolent Coordinating Committee speaks at a news conference.

in North Carolina aimed to use nonviolent action to free all Americans from **discrimination**.

There was still much opposition to desegregating schools, but change did slowly come. By the early 1980s, the state had some of the most racially integrated schools in the country, thanks to key court rulings of the 1960s and 1970s. African American students were attending schools and colleges of their choice throughout the state. North Carolinians of both races took pride as their state became one of the leaders in the southern movement toward equality. Important political changes arrived in North Carolina after 1968, with black mayors being elected in cities such as Durham, Raleigh, and Chapel Hill.

WORD TO KNOW

discrimination *unequal treatment based on race, gender, religion, or other factors*

A chemist conducts a cancer study at Research Triangle Park.

WORD TO KNOW

pharmaceutical *relating to the manufacture and sale of drugs used in medicine*

THE LATE 20TH CENTURY

A new industry began growing in the 1960s in North Carolina: scientific research. Business and government leaders helped establish Research Triangle Park, comprising three universities—Duke in Durham, North Carolina State (NCSU) in Raleigh, and the University of North Carolina (UNC) in Chapel Hill. It opened in 1959, stretching out across a large area among the three cities, and helped connect university scientists with industries. Attracted by this concentration of brainpower, many technology and **pharmaceutical** companies began moving to the area. Using the university scientists, these companies develop state-of-the-art products and systems.

The Democratic Party had dominated state politics since 1900. But that began to change in the 1970s. In 1972, voters elected James Holshouser Jr. as their first Republican governor since 1896. That same year, they elected Jesse Helms as their first Republican U.S. senator since 1895. Both Helms and North Carolina's Democratic senator Sam Ervin were prominent, outspoken members of Congress.

Many of the state's traditional industries suffered in the 1980s and 1990s. Tobacco continued to be North Carolina's major crop. But as more Americans learned about the health hazards of smoking, the tobacco industry declined. The textile and furniture industries experienced setbacks as well, because of competition from foreign-made goods.

Still, North Carolina's new industries are attracting talented people into the state—and employing thousands of longtime residents, too. Meanwhile, North Carolina's school system produces graduates who can spur the economy. In 2007, the business magazine *Forbes* named North Carolina the best place in the nation to do business or start a career. All in all, North Carolina seems well-prepared to meet the challenges of the 21st century.

MINI-BIO

ELIZABETH DOLE: NORTH CAROLINA'S FIRST FEMALE SENATOR

In 2002, Elizabeth Hanford Dole (1936–) became the first woman from North Carolina ever elected to the U.S. Senate. Before that, she had quite a busy career. She served as U.S. secretary of transportation (1983–1987), U.S. secretary of labor (1989–1990), and president of the American Red Cross (1991–1999). She was born in Salisbury and attended Duke University. At first, she was a Democrat, but she switched to the Republican Party in 1975.

? Want to know more? See http://dole.senate.gov/public/index.cfm?FuseAction=AboutElizabeth.Biography

72

READ ABOUT

Students and their teacher at a Greensboro middle school

CHAPTER SIX

PEOPLE

★

N ORTH CAROLINA'S PEOPLE HAVE INHERITED DIVERSE CULTURES. Those who live along the coast look back to a long seafaring tradition. In the western mountains, people preserve the folk music and crafts of their ancestors. Residents of the central Piedmont are near big-city centers for education, culture, sports, and the arts. And a wide variety of ethnic groups add to the state's rich cultural heritage.

A family in Chapel Hill

People QuickFacts

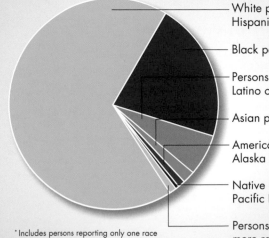

White persons not Hispanic: 68.3%

Black persons: 21.8%*

Persons of Hispanic or Latino origin: 6.4%†

Asian persons: 1.8%*

American Indian and Alaska Native persons: 1.3%*

Native Hawaiian and Other Pacific Islanders: 0.1%*

Persons reporting two or more races: 1.0%

* Includes persons reporting only one race
† Hispanics may be of any race, so they also are included in applicable race categories
Source: U.S. Census Bureau, 2005 estimate

MULTICULTURAL NORTH CAROLINA

North Carolinians trace their roots to countries all over the world. People with European ancestors make up the state's largest ethnic groups. Most are descended from English, German, Irish, Italian, and Scottish people. Many people in the Winston-Salem area have German ancestors. They are descendants of Moravian settlers who poured into the area in the 1700s. The Moravians were members of the Moravian Church, a Protestant group. Most had originally settled in Pennsylvania.

African Americans make up the state's second-largest group. More than one-fifth of all North Carolinians are African American. Most live in the coastal and Piedmont areas, and African American communities thrive in the northeast and south-central regions. Big cities also have large African American neighborhoods.

Hispanics, or Latinos, make up about 6 percent of the population. They are people whose original homelands are Spanish-speaking countries. North Carolina's Hispanic people are mostly from Mexico, Central America, Cuba, Puerto Rico, and the Dominican Republic. Between 1990 and 2000, the state's Hispanic population grew more than 400 percent.

Asian Americans—from China, Japan, Korea, India, Laos, Vietnam, among other Asian countries—make up less than 2 percent of the state's population. Between 1990 and 2002, the state's Asian American population grew 265 percent, with people from India and Vietnam making up the fastest-growing sector.

Only five states have larger Native American populations than North Carolina. Still, Native Americans make up less than 1.5 percent of the state's population. Several hundred thousand Native Americans once called North Carolina home. Today, only about 100,000 remain. The largest group is the Lumbee people, who live mainly in south-central North Carolina. The Eastern Band of Cherokee Indians is another large group. Most of them live in and around a region called the Qualla Boundary bordering Great Smoky Mountains National Park in the western mountains.

THE LUMBEE PEOPLE

North Carolina's Lumbee people are believed to be descended from many small Native American groups that banded together for safety in the 1700s. Their ancestry includes white and African American people. They hid in the swamps along the Lumber, or Lumbee, River. Today, the Lumbee people number more than 58,000, with most living in Robeson County. They make up the largest Native American nation east of the Mississippi River. Lumbees have no surviving language, but they speak a dialect called Lumbee English.

Where North Carolinians Live

The colors on this map indicate population density throughout the state. The darker the color, the more people live there.

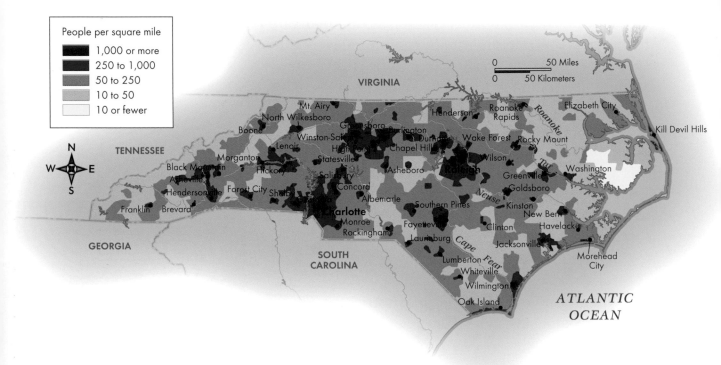

People per square mile
- 1,000 or more
- 250 to 1,000
- 50 to 250
- 10 to 50
- 10 or fewer

VIRGINIA

TENNESSEE

GEORGIA

SOUTH CAROLINA

ATLANTIC OCEAN

Mt. Airy
North Wilkesboro
Boone
Winston-Salem
Greensboro
Burlington
Henderson
Roanoke Rapids
Elizabeth City
Kill Devil Hills
Durham
Wake Forest
Rocky Mount
High Point
Chapel Hill
Lenoir
Statesville
Morganton
Black Mountain
Hickory
Asheville
Salisbury
Asheboro
Raleigh
Wilson
Greenville
Washington
Hendersonville
Forest City
Shelby
Concord
Goldsboro
Franklin
Brevard
Charlotte
Albemarle
Southern Pines
Kinston
New Bern
Monroe
Fayetteville
Clinton
Havelock
Rockingham
Laurinburg
Jacksonville
Lumberton
Whiteville
Morehead City
Wilmington
Oak Island

0   50 Miles
0   50 Kilometers

N W E S

Roanoke
Neuse
Tar
Cape Fear

Big City Life

This list shows the population of North Carolina's biggest cities.

Charlotte 630,478
Raleigh 356,321
Greensboro 236,865
Durham 209,009
Winston-Salem 196,990

Source: U.S. Census Bureau, 2006 estimate

EDUCATION

North Carolinians from 7 to 16 years old are required to attend school. About 8 percent of the state's students attend private schools.

North Carolina's universities are known worldwide for their quality of instruction and their research facilities. Opened in 1795, the University of North Carolina (UNC) at Chapel Hill was the nation's first public university. It grew to become one of the universities in North Carolina's Research Triangle Park, along with Duke University in Durham and North Carolina State

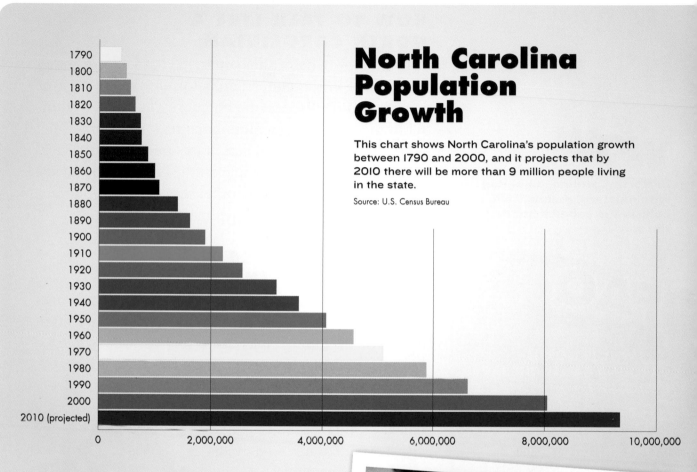

North Carolina Population Growth

This chart shows North Carolina's population growth between 1790 and 2000, and it projects that by 2010 there will be more than 9 million people living in the state.

Source: U.S. Census Bureau

University (NCSU) in Raleigh. Because these schools were clustered in this area, businesses that relied on research began locating there.

Today, the state university system includes 16 campuses. North Carolina has many private universities, too. The best-known are Duke University, Wake Forest University in Winston-Salem, Davidson College in Davidson, and Shaw University in Raleigh.

A music student

FAQ ★ ★ ★

Q8 WHY IS NORTH CAROLINA CALLED THE TAR HEEL STATE?

A8 There are many legends explaining this nickname. One popular story comes from the time of the Civil War (1861–1865). It was said that the North Carolina soldiers stuck to their fighting as if they had tar on their heels, which, perhaps, referred to the naval stores their home state was known for at the time. As the story goes, their commander, General Robert E. Lee, said, "God bless the Tar-heel boys!"

HOW TO TALK LIKE A NORTH CAROLINIAN

Do you know what a dingbatter is? That's a term sometimes used in the Outer Banks to refer to a tourist or outsider. And what about a boomer? That's a red squirrel in the Appalachian Mountains region. If something is crooked, people in the mountains might say it's sigogglin (SYE-gog-lin), but people on the coast might say it's cattywampus. Like many southerners, North Carolinians often address two or more people as "y'all."

HOW TO EAT LIKE A NORTH CAROLINIAN

Some of North Carolinians' favorite foods are their own local products. Chicken, turkey, and hog products often end up on the dinner table. Crops such as sweet potatoes, peanuts, and blueberries are favorites, too. Along the coast, people enjoy fresh seafood. They prepare deep-fried fish, roasted oysters, and boiled blue crabs. Immigrants also brought their food traditions to the state. Moravian settlers introduced some delicious cookies, cakes, and buns that are still being baked there today.

Oysters with cocktail sauce

MENU

WHAT'S ON THE MENU IN NORTH CAROLINA?

Livermush

People in central North Carolina love livermush! It's a mixture of pig parts, cornmeal, and spices. It's high in protein and low in fat. The mayor of Shelby has called livermush "the world's most perfect food." It's believed that German settlers brought it to the region. Today, people enjoy livermush as a fried breakfast meat, in sandwiches or omelets, and even as a pizza topping!

Barbecue—East or West?

Barbecued pork, made from a pig or hog, is a North Carolina taste treat. But the eastern and western parts of the state have different barbecue styles. In the east, the whole animal is barbecued. The sauce is made of vinegar, water, salt, and pepper. Western-style barbecue uses only the shoulder of the animal. The sauce is similar to the eastern style, but with tomatoes and a little brown sugar added.

Moravian Sweets

Moravian baked goods are especially popular around Christmastime. Favorite holiday treats include thin, crispy wafers called spice crisps. They may be flavored with cinnamon, ginger, nutmeg, and other spices. Sugar cake is popular, too. It's a square cake with brown sugar and spices on top.

TRY THIS RECIPE
Sweet Potato Smoothies

The sweet potato is North Carolina's official state vegetable. North Carolinians use sweet potatoes to make bread, muffins, crackers, cake, pie, pudding, and even salsa. Try this recipe for sweet potato smoothies. They're delicious, nutritious, and easy to make! (Be sure to have an adult nearby in case you need help.)

Ingredients:
1 medium sweet potato
1 cup frozen vanilla yogurt
1 cup orange juice
½ teaspoon vanilla extract

Instructions:
1. Boil the sweet potato until it's soft (about 30 minutes).
2. When it's cool, peel it and mash it up in a bowl.
3. Refrigerate the mashed sweet potato for about 2 hours, or until it's completely cold.
4. Place the mashed sweet potato and all the other ingredients in a blender. Blend on high until the mixture is smooth.
5. Serve at once or refrigerate. Makes two 8-ounce servings.

Sweet potatoes

MINI-BIO

BETSY BYARS: SHE JUST KEPT TRYING

Betsy Byars (1928—) never imagined she'd be a writer. When she finally tried writing, her first children's book was rejected nine times before being published. Now the Charlotte native is the award-winning author of more than 50 books for young readers. Her novel *Summer of the Swans* won the Newbery Medal, and *The Night Swimmers* won a National Book Award. Her popular books include the Bingo Brown, Blossom Family, Golly Sisters, and Herculeah Jones series.

 Want to know more? See www.edupaperback. org/showauth.cfm?authid=19

Asheville native Thomas Wolfe

NORTH CAROLINA WRITERS

The clever stories of one North Carolina author have been entertaining readers for more than 100 years. O. Henry was the pen name of William Sydney Porter, a master short-story writer. Henry's "The Ransom of Red Chief" is the hilarious tale of a kidnapped boy who ends up terrorizing his kidnappers. Thomas Wolfe of Asheville was one of the great American novelists of the 20th century. His novel *Look Homeward, Angel* recounts the life of a boy growing up in a town much like Asheville.

North Carolina has been home to many authors of books for children and young adults. Theodore

Taylor is best known for *The Cay*, the story of a young white boy and an elderly black man who are shipwrecked together. Charlotte native Betsy Byars is the author of many popular books for young adults, including *Summer of the Swans* and the Blossom Family series. Shelia P. Moses wrote *The Legend of Buddy Bush* and other novels. They reflect the racial discrimination she experienced as a child in Rich Square. Sarah Dessen, who grew up in Chapel Hill, wrote *Just Listen* and several other young-adult novels.

THE ARTS SCENE

North Carolina was the first state to form its own orchestra. Today, the Raleigh-based North Carolina Symphony presents concerts around the state, including free afternoon performances for kids. Several other cities have orchestras, too. North Carolina was also the first state whose government set aside funds to purchase a collection of art for the public to enjoy. That art is now displayed in the North Carolina Museum of Art in Raleigh.

Duke University hosts the American Dance Festival every summer. In the 1980s, this festival hosted a dance group that became the African American Dance Ensemble. Now a professional dance company, it offers African and African American dance performances throughout the state.

MINI-BIO

SHELIA P. MOSES: STORIES OF STRUGGLE

Born and raised in Rich Square, Shelia P. Moses (1961–) was the ninth of ten children. She drew on her childhood experiences for her young-adult novels *The Legend of Buddy Bush*, *The Return of Buddy Bush*, and *The Baptism*. Her stories focus on discrimination and the struggle for racial equality. *The Legend of Buddy Bush*, a Coretta Scott King Honor Book, is told from the point of view of a 12-year-old girl living in a small town in North Carolina in the 1940s.

? **Want to know more?** See http://biography. jrank.org/pages/2154/Moses-Sheila-P-1961.html

An audience watches a performance of *The Lost Colony* on Roanoke Island.

The Andy Griffith Show and Mayberry R.F.D., though filmed in California, were set in the fictional town of Mayberry, North Carolina. The town is based on Mount Airy, the actual hometown of actor Andy Griffith.

North Carolina is also known for its historical dramas, which are held outdoors in the summertime. *The Lost Colony* is presented in Manteo on Roanoke Island. It portrays Sir Walter Raleigh's founding of the Roanoke Colony in the 1580s and the colony's mysterious disappearance. *Unto These Hills* shows the plight of the Cherokee people as they were removed from their homeland and forced along the Trail of Tears. It's staged in the town of Cherokee, with Cherokee actors.

North Carolinians enjoy a rich heritage of folk culture, and folk arts are still very much alive there. Some craftspeople still lovingly carve musical instruments from wood. They make fiddles, banjos, and dulcimers (the dulcimer is a stringed instrument with a long, narrow body). Other North Carolina craftspeople carve chairs and other furniture from wood. Popular textile crafts in the state range from spinning and weaving cotton or wool to making multicolored quilts. Pottery making is another important craft tradition in the region. North Carolina's Native Americans create beautiful craftwork, too. They use centuries-old designs to make pottery, baskets, jewelry, masks, weapons, and carved gourds.

North Carolina is known for its many traditional music styles, including folk music, bluegrass, blues, and country. In the 1700s, people from England, Scotland, and Ireland settled in the western mountains. They brought their songs and dances with them. Today, this traditional music lives on through fiddling, banjo-picking, ballads, dancing, and other art forms.

SPORTS

North Carolina has four professional sports teams. In football, it's the Charlotte-based Carolina Panthers. In men's basketball, it's the Charlotte Bobcats, and in women's basketball, it's the Charlotte Sting. And Raleigh's Carolina Hurricanes are the state's hockey team. The Hurricanes won the Stanley Cup, hockey's championship, in 2006.

North Carolinians are wild about college sports, especially basketball. Fans take sides in the fierce basketball competition between UNC–Chapel Hill and Duke. Basketball superstar Michael Jordan grew up in Wilmington and got his start playing for the North Carolina

Q8 WHAT IS THE ORIGIN OF THE BANJO?

A8 West African people made stringed instruments using gourds, wood, twine, and animal hides. When Africans were brought to the Americas as slaves, they fashioned a similar musical instrument called the *mbanza* out of available materials. This eventually developed into the banjo.

MINI-BIO

MICHAEL JORDAN: BASKETBALL SUPERSTAR

Michael Jordan (1963–) is one of the greatest basketball players of all time. His leaping ability wowed fans, earning him the nickname "Air Jordan." Born in New York, he moved with his family to Wilmington at age seven. He won a basketball scholarship to UNC–Chapel Hill, and in 1982 he made the game-winning shot that won the Tar Heels the National Collegiate Athletic Association (NCAA) title. Jordan soon joined the Chicago Bulls and led them to six National Basketball Association (NBA) championships.

❓ Want to know more? See http://statelibrary.dcr. state.nc.us/nc/bio/sports/sports.htm

The Duke Blue Devils take on the Universty of North Carolina Tar Heels at the Dean Smith Center in Chapel HIll.

MINI-BIO

MIA HAMM: SOCCER GREAT

Soccer champ Mia Hamm (1972–) began playing organized soccer at age 5, and at age 15, she became the youngest woman ever to play on the U.S. national team. At UNC–Chapel Hill (1989–1993), she helped her team win four championships. On the U.S. women's Olympic soccer team, she won gold medals in 1996 and 2004 and the silver medal in 2000. Over the course of her career, Hamm scored 158 goals in international games. No other soccer player, male or female, has scored that many. Though she retired in 2004, she continues to serve as a role model for girls around the world.

? Want to know more? See www.soccerhall.org/famers/mia_hamm.htm

Tar Heels. That's the name for all the athletic teams at UNC–Chapel Hill. In the 1990s, Tar Heel fans thrilled to the moves of Mia Hamm, perhaps the greatest female soccer player ever. That team has won more national women's soccer championships than any other school.

Car racing is another popular sport in North Carolina. In fact, North Carolina is home to more than 80 percent of the racing teams in the National Association for Stock Car Auto Racing (NASCAR). Top races take place at speedways in Charlotte, Asheville, Winston-Salem, Hickory, and North Wilkesboro. Two North

Carolina families are local racing legends. One is the Petty family. Richard Petty, born in Level Cross, won the NASCAR championship seven times. The Richard Petty Museum in Randleman exhibits his cars and traces his racing history. Richard Petty's father, Lee, was a well-known racer, and so is Richard's son, Kyle.

The Earnhardts are another racing family. Ralph Earnhardt, Dale Earnhardt Sr., and Dale Earnhardt Jr. were all born in Kannapolis. Ralph started the family tradition when he switched from working at a cotton mill to racing. Dale Sr., who died in a 2001 racing crash, is tied with Richard Petty for the most NASCAR championships. Now Dale Jr. continues the Earnhardt legacy as a top-notch racer. Like the state's musicians and craftspeople, racers hand down their skills from one generation to another to keep their proud traditions alive.

Fans watch the start of the Coca-Cola 600 race at the Lowe's Motor Speedway in Charlotte.

MINI-BIO

RICHARD PETTY: KING OF RACING

Racing great Richard Petty (1937–), nicknamed "the King," won seven NASCAR championships and holds the records for the most wins in a row (10) and most wins in a single season (27). Petty survived many crashes in his career. After retiring in 1992, he was awarded the Presidential Medal of Freedom.

? Want to know more? See www.clemson.edu/autoresearch/ASRI/biorichardpetty.html

READ ABOUT

A school group on the grounds of the capitol in Raleigh

CHAPTER SEVEN

GOVERNMENT

★

WHEN STUDENTS AT WILSON'S ELVIE STREET SCHOOL FOUND THAT THEIR STATE HAD NO OFFICIAL VEGETABLE, THEY SET TO WORK. They knew that North Carolina produces more sweet potatoes than almost any other state. So they researched how laws are made. Then they wrote letters to their state lawmakers, made phone calls, and got their community involved in the effort. In 1995, the lawmakers passed a law that declared the sweet potato North Carolina's official state vegetable.

The state capitol in Raleigh

THE NORTH CAROLINA CONSTITUTION

Like the U.S. government, North Carolina's state government is divided into three branches—the legislative, executive, and judicial branches. This three-way division was outlined in North Carolina's first constitution, adopted in 1776. A second constitution was drafted in 1868. The present constitution went into effect in 1971, and it can still be amended, or changed. State lawmakers can propose a change, and three-fifths of them must approve it. Then a majority of the voters must approve the amendment.

Capitol Facts

Here are some fascinating facts about North Carolina's state capitol.

Number of stories high 3
Structure on top . . . . .Copper dome
Height from floor to dome. . . . . .97.5 feet (30 m)
North–south (left to right) measurement . . . . . 160 feet (49 m)
East–west (front to back) measurement . . . . . . 140 feet (43 m)
Construction dates 1833–1840

Capital City

This map shows places of interest in Raleigh, North Carolina's capital city.

THE STATE CAPITOL

As you enter the capitol, you walk into the rotunda—the wide-open area beneath the dome. In the center is a statue of George Washington dressed like an ancient Roman general. Around the rotunda are plaques and statues honoring people in North Carolina's history. On the second floor are the two chambers where the General Assembly used to meet. They are designed to resemble ancient Greek public buildings. The third floor once housed the state library and the state geologist's office, which held a "cabinet of minerals" collected from throughout the state.

THE LEGISLATIVE BRANCH

The job of the legislative branch is to make laws. North Carolina's legislature, or lawmaking body, is called the General Assembly. Like the U.S. Congress, it's divided into two chambers, or houses—the 50-member senate and the 120-member house of representatives. The General Assembly used to meet in the capitol but now meets in the state legislative building one block away.

It cost $532,682.34 to build the capitol, which was completed in 1840. Today, that would amount to more than $11.4 million!

North Carolina State Government

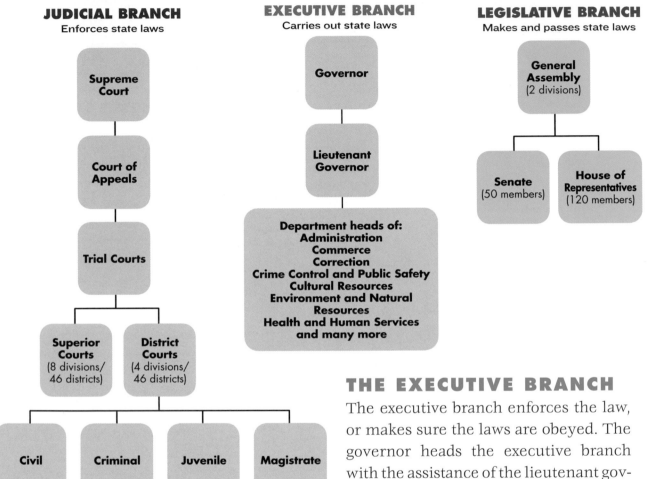

JUDICIAL BRANCH
Enforces state laws

- Supreme Court
- Court of Appeals
- Trial Courts
  - Superior Courts (8 divisions/ 46 districts)
  - District Courts (4 divisions/ 46 districts)
    - Civil
    - Criminal
    - Juvenile
    - Magistrate

EXECUTIVE BRANCH
Carries out state laws

- Governor
- Lieutenant Governor
- Department heads of:
  Administration
  Commerce
  Correction
  Crime Control and Public Safety
  Cultural Resources
  Environment and Natural Resources
  Health and Human Services
  and many more

LEGISLATIVE BRANCH
Makes and passes state laws

- General Assembly (2 divisions)
  - Senate (50 members)
  - House of Representatives (120 members)

THE EXECUTIVE BRANCH

The executive branch enforces the law, or makes sure the laws are obeyed. The governor heads the executive branch with the assistance of the lieutenant governor. Several executive officers oversee various specialized departments. They include the secretary of state, the state treasurer, the state auditor, the attorney general, and the heads of the agriculture, insurance, and labor departments.

THE JUDICIAL BRANCH

The judicial branch of government consists of judges. Their job is to apply the

Representing North Carolina

This list shows the number of elected officials who represent North Carolina, both on the state and national levels.

OFFICE	NUMBER	LENGTH OF TERM
State senators	50	2 years
State representatives	120	2 years
U.S. senators	2	6 years
U.S. representatives	13	2 years
Presidential electors	15	—

WEIRD LAWS

North Carolina has some pretty wacky laws. Some are simply old laws that remain on the books but are no longer enforced. Others are the unintended result of poorly written laws.

- Elephants may not be used to plow cotton fields.
- Bingo games may not last more than five hours unless they are held at a fair.
- It's against the law to sing off-key.
- In Charlotte, women must cover their bodies with 16 yards (15 m) of cloth at all times.
- In Asheville, it's illegal to sneeze on city streets.

MINI-BIO

JOHN EDWARDS: FROM POVERTY TO POLITICS

John Edwards (1953–) grew up in a poor family in Robbins and became a prominent Raleigh attorney. After his son Wade died in 1996, he decided to go into politics. He served as a U.S. senator from North Carolina (1999–2005). In 2004, he ran as the Democratic vice presidential candidate with John Kerry, but they lost. In 2008, Edwards made an unsuccessful run for the Democratic presidential nomination, with global warming and universal health care among his major issues.

 Want to know more? See www.pbs.org/ newshour/vote2008/primaries/candidates/ edwards.html

NORTH CAROLINIANS IN THE WHITE HOUSE

Andrew Jackson (1767–1845) was the seventh president of the United States (1829–1837). He was born near the border of North and South Carolina, possibly in Waxhaw. His victory at the Battle of New Orleans during the War of 1812 made him a national hero.

James K. Polk (1795–1849) was the 11th president of the United States (1845–1849). Born in Pineville, North Carolina, he spent most of his life in Tennessee.

Andrew Johnson (1808–1875) was the 17th president of the United States (1865–1869). Born in Raleigh, he served during the Reconstruction period after the Civil War. Congress tried twice to impeach him but failed.

92

MINI-BIO

HENRY FRYE: CHIEF JUSTICE

After growing up on a farm in Ellerbe, Henry Frye (1932–) served in the U.S. Air Force. But he was denied the right to vote because he didn't pass a literacy test. This test required that a voter be able to read and understand the Constitution. Whites who registered voters denied most blacks the right to vote by saying they didn't understand the document. This injustice inspired Frye to become an attorney. He also served in the General Assembly for many years. He became the first African American on North Carolina's supreme court, serving as associate justice (1983–1999) and chief justice (1999–2001).

? Want to know more? See www.unctv.org/bif/transcripts/1999/bif1520.html

law. That is, they listen to cases in their courts and decide whether someone has broken a law. The Supreme Court of North Carolina is the state's highest court. It's composed of a chief justice, or judge, and six associate justices. The court of appeals is the next-highest court. Its 15 judges take turns presiding over the court in groups of three.

Next come the superior courts and the district courts. Superior courts handle serious crimes, and district courts deal with lesser crimes.

One North Carolina trailblazer was Susie Sharp. She was elected the first female chief justice of the state supreme court in 1974. She served on the court for 12 years and was one of *Time* magazine's women of the year in 1975.

LOCAL GOVERNMENT

North Carolina is divided into 100 counties. Each county is governed by a three- to seven-member board of commissioners. Depending on the county, voters elect the commissioners to two-year or four-year terms. Voters also elect county officers such as the sheriff and the county attorney.

Most of North Carolina's larger cities and towns elect a city manager and a city council. Other cities and towns may elect a mayor and city council or a

Susie Sharp

town commission. North Carolina also has more than 500 small towns and villages that are unincorporated. That means they do not have their own government because they are too small to need one. Instead, they are governed by the county.

North Carolina Counties

This map shows the 100 counties in North Carolina. Raleigh, the state capital, is indicated with a star.

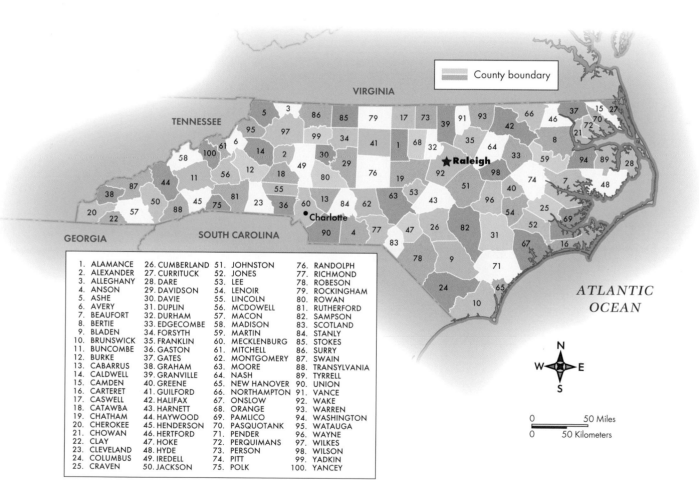

1. ALAMANCE
2. ALEXANDER
3. ALLEGHANY
4. ANSON
5. ASHE
6. AVERY
7. BEAUFORT
8. BERTIE
9. BLADEN
10. BRUNSWICK
11. BUNCOMBE
12. BURKE
13. CABARRUS
14. CALDWELL
15. CAMDEN
16. CARTERET
17. CASWELL
18. CATAWBA
19. CHATHAM
20. CHEROKEE
21. CHOWAN
22. CLAY
23. CLEVELAND
24. COLUMBUS
25. CRAVEN
26. CUMBERLAND
27. CURRITUCK
28. DARE
29. DAVIDSON
30. DAVIE
31. DUPLIN
32. DURHAM
33. EDGECOMBE
34. FORSYTH
35. FRANKLIN
36. GASTON
37. GATES
38. GRAHAM
39. GRANVILLE
40. GREENE
41. GUILFORD
42. HALIFAX
43. HARNETT
44. HAYWOOD
45. HENDERSON
46. HERTFORD
47. HOKE
48. HYDE
49. IREDELL
50. JACKSON
51. JOHNSTON
52. JONES
53. LEE
54. LENOIR
55. LINCOLN
56. MCDOWELL
57. MACON
58. MADISON
59. MARTIN
60. MECKLENBURG
61. MITCHELL
62. MONTGOMERY
63. MOORE
64. NASH
65. NEW HANOVER
66. NORTHAMPTON
67. ONSLOW
68. ORANGE
69. PAMLICO
70. PASQUOTANK
71. PENDER
72. PERQUIMANS
73. PERSON
74. PITT
75. POLK
76. RANDOLPH
77. RICHMOND
78. ROBESON
79. ROCKINGHAM
80. ROWAN
81. RUTHERFORD
82. SAMPSON
83. SCOTLAND
84. STANLY
85. STOKES
86. SURRY
87. SWAIN
88. TRANSYLVANIA
89. TYRRELL
90. UNION
91. VANCE
92. WAKE
93. WARREN
94. WASHINGTON
95. WATAUGA
96. WAYNE
97. WILKES
98. WILSON
99. YADKIN
100. YANCEY

State Flag

The state flag was adopted in 1885. It has a blue vertical stripe on the left. In the center of the stripe is a white star, with the letter N on its left and the letter C on its right. Above the star is the date May 20th, 1775. This is the date of the so-called Mecklenburg Declaration of Independence, a strong anti-British statement from the people of Mecklenburg County. Most historians do not believe that the Mecklenburg Declaration of Independence is real, however. Below the star is the date when North Carolinians told their delegates to the Continental Congress to vote for independence—April 12th, 1776.

State Seal

The state seal, adopted in 1984, also bears the dates that are on the state flag. The standing figure on the seal represents Liberty and the seated figure depicts Plenty. The North Carolina mountains and coast provide a backdrop. Also included is the state motto, *Esse quam videri*, which means "To be, rather than to seem."

READ ABOUT

Medical
researchers at
Duke University
in Durham

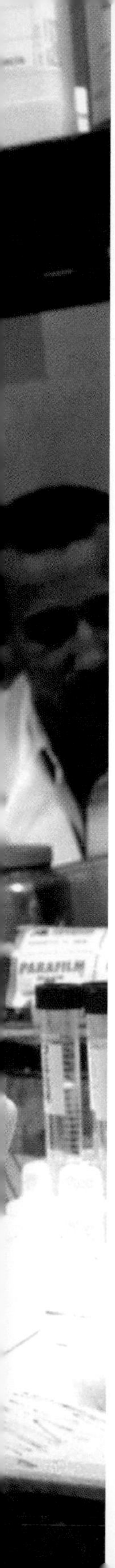

CHAPTER EIGHT

ECONOMY

★

NORTH CAROLINA HAS COME A LONG WAY SINCE THE 1700s AND 1800s, WHEN AGRICULTURE WAS ITS MAJOR INDUSTRY. Now the state is a leader in banking, furniture making, medical research, and high-technology industries. Many objects you see every day—chairs, bricks, paper, and medicines—are North Carolina products. Agriculture is still a major industry, though. From sweet potatoes to pigs and turkeys, North Carolina raises more than almost any other state!

Doctors and nurses are among the many service workers who contribute to North Carolina's economy.

SERVICE INDUSTRIES

North Carolina's top industry group is services. Service industries involve people and companies that sell helpful services, rather than manufacturing goods or growing crops. People who teach school, repair bikes, or drive trucks are all service industry workers.

Some of the state's leading services are financial services, health care, and scientific research. Bank of

America and Wachovia Bank, two of the nation's largest banks, are headquartered in Charlotte. Research Triangle Park, between Raleigh and Durham, is an important research center. Scientists there conduct experiments to create new products for medical, electronics, and other industries. North Carolina has one of the largest **biotechnology** industries in the nation, and many new drugs are developed there.

Real estate, or the sale of land and buildings, is another big service industry. Many North Carolinians work in wholesale and retail trade. Retailers are companies that sell goods directly to the public. Your local grocery store, for example, is a retail store. So are all the shops in a mall. Lowe's is a large retailer based in Mooresville. It distributes home improvement products to stores nationwide. Wholesalers are companies that sell goods to the retailers.

Tourism services include hotels, lodges, camping outfitters, and ferryboats for vacationers. The Tidewater and the mountains are the major tourist regions. North Carolina also has a little-known but growing filmmaking industry.

Government is another large service industry in the state. Public schools, national and state parks, and military bases all provide government services. North Carolina's military bases include Camp Lejeune Marine Corps Base in Jacksonville and Fort Bragg Army post in Fayetteville.

WORD TO KNOW

biotechnology *the manipulation of living organisms for developments in the areas of food production, waste disposal, mining, and medicine*

FAQ

Q: WHAT ARE SOME FACTS ABOUT RESEARCH TRIANGLE PARK?

A: Land area: 7,000 acres (2,833 hectares)
Number of companies: 157
Number of employees: More than 39,000
Total salaries: More than $2.7 billion
Largest employers: International Business Machines (IBM; information technology) and GlaxoSmithKline (drugs)
Recreation: More than 14 miles (23 km) of trails, 12 volleyball courts, and 4 softball diamonds

SEE IT HERE!

BLUE RIDGE MOTION PICTURES

Go behind the scenes to see how movies are made when you tour Asheville's Blue Ridge Motion Pictures. As you tour the studio, you'll walk through the soundstages, including the "wet stage," where water effects are filmed. In the art department, you'll see people at work building models and painting scenery. On the back lot, you'll see where street scenes are shot. At the end, you'll watch *The History of Movies*, a film about a century of moviemaking.

Top Products

Agriculture Broilers, hogs, greenhouse and nursery products, turkeys, tobacco

Manufacturing Chemical products, tobacco products, food products, furniture

Mining Crushed stone, phosphate rock, sand and gravel, feldspar

Fishing Blue crabs, shrimp, flounder, menhaden, clams

What Do North Carolinians Do?

This color-coded chart shows what industries North Carolinians work in.

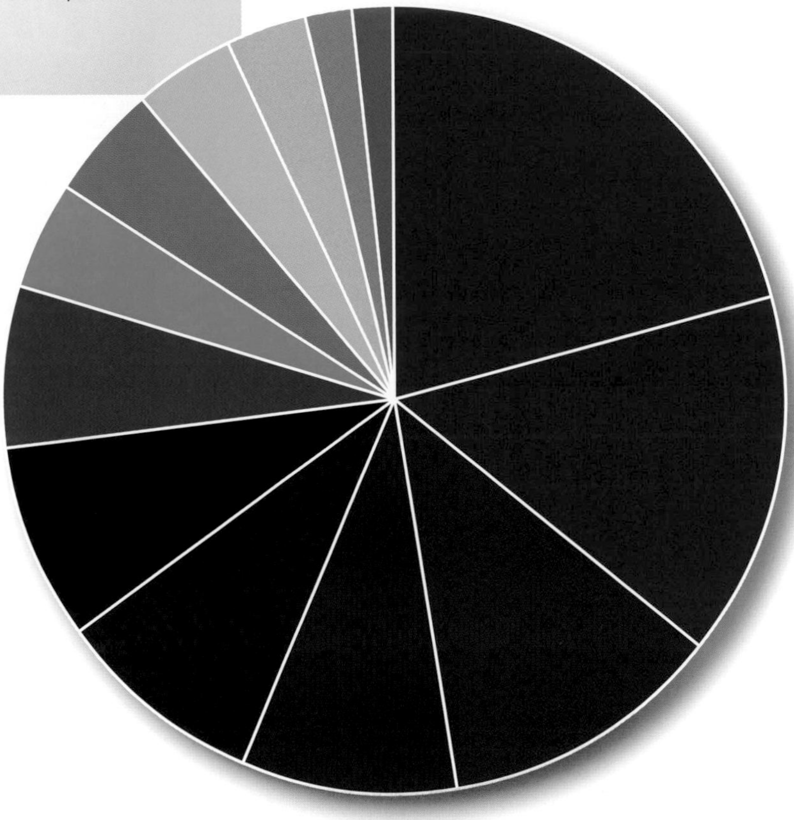

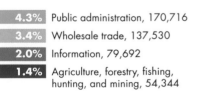

21.0% Educational services, health care, and social assistance, 837,684

14.9% Manufacturing, 594,364

11.6% Retail trade, 463,038

9.0% Construction, 361,307

8.7% Professional, scientific, management, administrative, and waste management services, 347,763

8.0% Arts, entertainment, recreation, accommodation, and food services, 320,896

6.6% Finance, insurance, real estate, rental, and leasing, 264,965

4.6% Other services, except public administration, 183,823

4.5% Transportation, warehousing, and utilities, 179,295

4.3% Public administration, 170,716

3.4% Wholesale trade, 137,530

2.0% Information, 79,692

1.4% Agriculture, forestry, fishing, hunting, and mining, 54,344

Source: U.S. Census Bureau, 2005 estimate

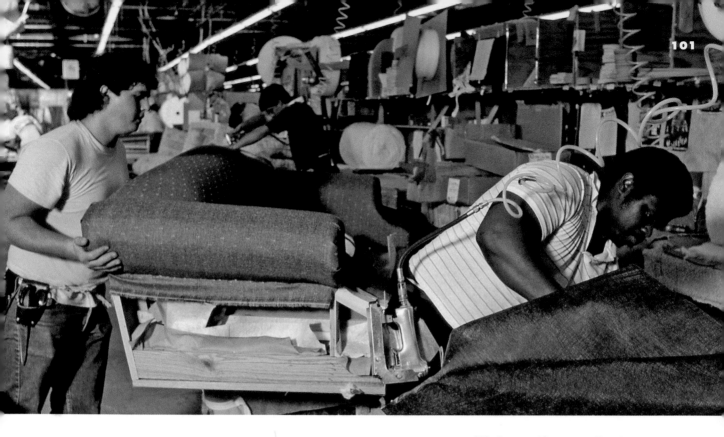

MANUFACTURING

Most of North Carolina's manufacturing industries are in the Piedmont. Chemicals and tobacco products are the state's leading manufactured goods. Chemical products made in North Carolina include cleansers, plastics, and pharmaceuticals, or drugs. North Carolina leads all other states in manufacturing tobacco products.

North Carolina is also a top producer of textiles (cloth) and wooden furniture. The textile industry has declined in recent years. Since the 1980s, foreign companies have been producing these goods more cheaply and selling them in the United States at lower prices than American-made goods.

North Carolina's furniture industry has thrived for centuries because of the state's abundant forests. The city of High Point has been called the Furniture Capital of the World. Twice a year, it hosts the High Point Market. This is the world's largest furniture industry trade show,

Workers at Klaussner Furniture, headquartered in Asheboro

with buyers and sellers from more than 100 countries. But foreign competition has hurt this industry, too, and dozens of furniture companies have shut down since 1995. Still, furniture remains an important industry in the state.

North Carolina's factories make many other valuable products. Some plants process and package canned foods, meat products, and soft drinks. Others make telephones and computer parts. Still others manufac-

Globalization versus Local Industry

In recent years, the governments and companies of many different countries have been cooperating in the area of trade. Companies from China sell their furniture in the United States, while companies in North Carolina might buy parts made in Mexico or hire workers based in India. This process is called globalization.

PRO

Many people believe globalization is a positive force because it helps improve conditions for people in underdeveloped countries. According to economist Jeffrey Sachs:

"Globalization gives developing countries an unprecedented opportunity to catch up with the more advanced economies. . . . Improving technologies and skills can raise living standards around the world."
—Jeffrey Sachs, *Globalization and Employment*, 1996; *The End of Poverty*, 2005

CON

Others believe that globalization comes at too high a cost to U.S. industries. According to a panel of North Carolina economists:

"Globalization is the primary reason for the dilemma currently faced by the furniture industry. . . . Chinese companies are producing high-quality goods at lower prices for sale in the U.S. . . . Hourly wages for furniture workers in China are between $0.50 and $0.75."
—*North Carolina and the Global Economy*, Spring 2004

ture industrial machinery such as jet engines, power tools, and construction equipment. Lumber mills make plywood and other building materials, and paper mills make many types of paper and cardboard.

AGRICULTURE

North Carolina is one of the richest agricultural states in the country. In 2005, it was the nation's second-largest producer of hogs, pigs, and turkeys and ranked third in chicken and egg products.

North Carolina leads all the states in growing tobacco. Other important crops include cotton, corn, soybeans, and peanuts. North Carolina is a major sweet potato producer, ranking first in the nation in

Cultivating a field of soybeans in Robeson County

Major Agricultural and Mining Products

This map shows where North Carolina's major agricultural and mining products come from. See a chicken? That means poultry is raised here.

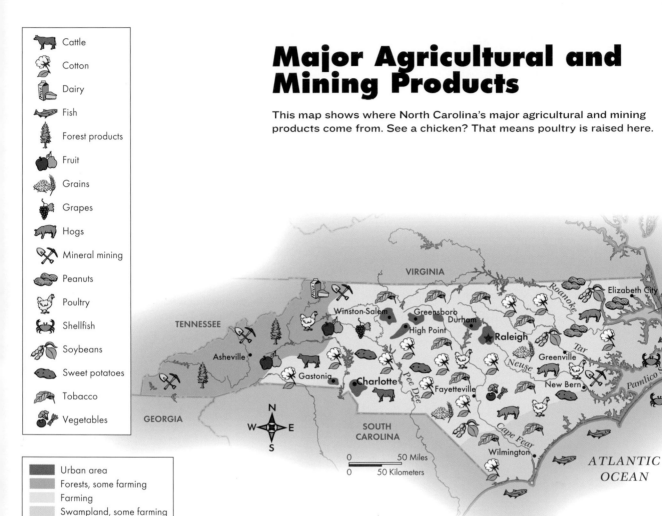

Cattle
Cotton
Dairy
Fish
Forest products
Fruit
Grains
Grapes
Hogs
Mineral mining
Peanuts
Poultry
Shellfish
Soybeans
Sweet potatoes
Tobacco
Vegetables

Urban area
Forests, some farming
Farming
Swampland, some farming

2005. Cucumbers, cabbage, bell peppers, squash, and tomatoes are some other important vegetable crops. Blueberries are the state's top fruit crop. Many North Carolina farmers also grow apples, peaches, strawberries, grapes, and watermelons.

FISHERIES AND MINING

With its long coastline, North Carolina has a thriving fishing industry. Flounder is the most valuable fish

Fishing boats in the Intracoastal Waterway, which runs all along the Atlantic coast

catch. Other important species are menhaden, croaker, tuna, and mackerel. Blue crabs are the most valuable shellfish catch, followed by shrimp. Fishers collect clams, oysters, and scallops offshore, too. Some North Carolinians run fish or shellfish farms. They raise trout, catfish, crayfish, and other popular species.

Most of North Carolina's mining products are minerals used in the construction industry. Crushed stone is the most valuable mineral, followed by phosphate rock, sand and gravel, feldspar, and dimension stone. The state's clays are made into all kinds of bricks, as well as floor tiles.

In 2007, the business magazine *Forbes* ranked five North Carolina cities among the top 25 cities in the country as the best places to do business or start a career. Those cities are Raleigh, Durham, Charlotte, Asheville, and Winston-Salem.

In 2003, the largest emerald ever found in North America was discovered at a mine in Hiddenite, in the west-central part of the state. It weighed 1,869 carats (13 ounces/369 grams). That's heavier than a can of soda!

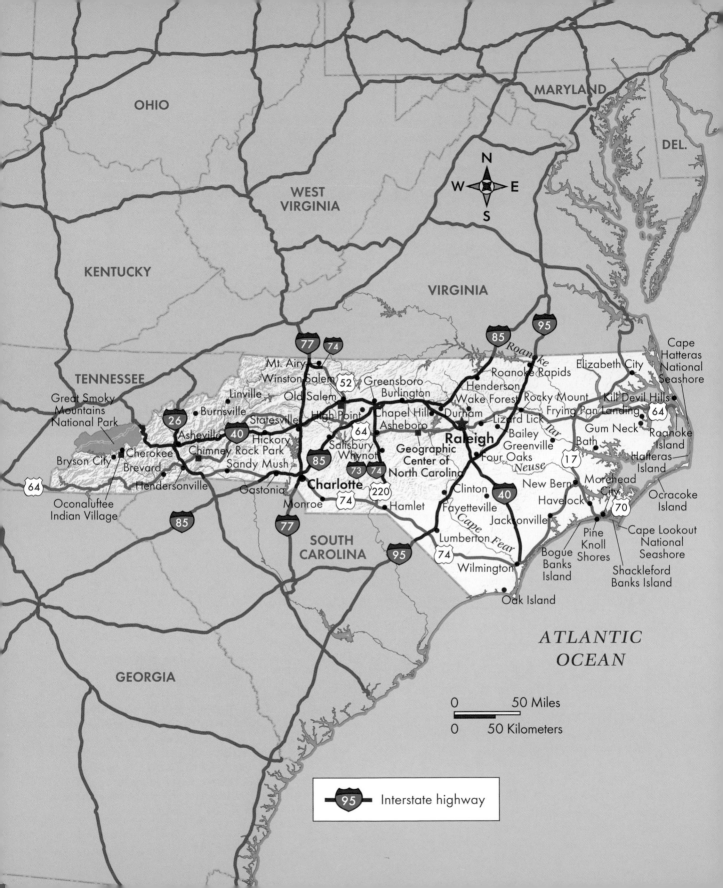

CHAPTER NINE

TRAVEL GUIDE

★

FROM ITS BEAUTIFUL BEACHES TO ITS MISTY MOUNTAIN PEAKS, NORTH CAROLINA IS FULL OF ADVENTURE AND FUN. Discover the wonders of wildlife, from black bears to sharks. Climb a rugged cliff or a towering lighthouse. Whether you enjoy the state on a road trip or curled up with a book at home, you'll find North Carolina is a great place to explore!

← Follow along with this travel map. We'll begin on Roanoke Island and travel all the way to Bryson City.

THE COAST

THINGS TO DO: See where the Wright brothers flew their plane, climb aboard a World War II battleship, explore Blackbeard's hideout, climb a lighthouse, or collect seashells along the shore.

Roanoke Island

★ **Fort Raleigh National Historic Site:** See where Sir Walter Raleigh sent England's first colonists in the 1580s. In summer, you can watch *The Lost Colony*, an outdoor drama about the colonists who disappeared without a trace.

Kill Devil Hills

★ **Wright Brothers National Memorial:** The Wright brothers made the first controlled, powered airplane flight in 1903 near Kitty Hawk. In the museum here, you can see a reproduction of the Wrights' 1903 airplane and their 1902 glider.

Wright Brothers National Memorial

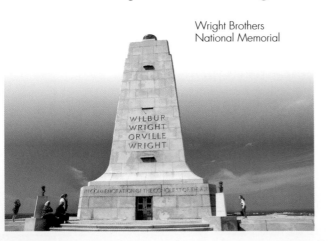

Swimming at Nags Head, Cape Hatteras

Cape Hatteras National Seashore

★ **Hatteras Island:** This narrow, 50-mile-long (80 km) island makes up the largest section of the Outer Banks. On the north end of the island, explore the hiking trails through Pea Island National Wildlife Refuge. You can also visit the Cape Hatteras Lighthouse, which was completed in 1870. At 207 feet (63 m), it's the tallest lighthouse in North America.

★ **Ocracoke Island:** Once a hideout of Blackbeard the pirate, this island lies southwest of Hatteras Island. On the island's east end, you can visit a herd of wild Ocracoke ponies at the National Park Service Pony Pen.

SEE IT HERE!

NORTH CAROLINA AQUARIUM AT PINE KNOLL SHORES

This aquarium sits along the shore at Atlantic Beach on Bogue Banks Island. Here you'll come eye-to-eye with turtles, eels, snakes, alligators, and dozens of colorful fish. Check out the diving shows, the live animal programs, and the touch tank. You can also talk to divers as they mingle with sharks in the huge Living Shipwreck water tank. Outdoor nature trails and a natural marsh are part of the complex, too.

Cape Lookout National Seashore

★ **Shackleford Banks Island:** More than 100 wild horses graze on this island. Keep your distance, though. They are wild and may kick if disturbed. Along the beaches, you can swim, fish, or collect seashells.

Bath

★ **Historic Bath:** When visiting North Carolina's first town, you can join a guided tour or just stroll around on your own. The Palmer-Marsh House, the Van Der Veer House, and the Bonner House—all built by early merchants, planters, and officials of Bath in the 1700s and 1800s—are open to visitors.

★ **Plum Point:** This stretch of land was the home of Edward Teach, better known as Blackbeard the pirate. Explore the site to find what are rumored to be the ruins of Blackbeard's home.

Gardens at Tryon Palace

New Bern

★ **Tryon Palace:** This elegant mansion was the home of North Carolina's royal governor, William Tryon. Costumed guides lead visitors on tours through the home and gardens. On the palace grounds, craftspeople demonstrate colonial crafts.

★ **Birthplace of Pepsi:** In this drugstore, at 256 Middle Street, Caleb Bradham invented Pepsi-Cola in 1898. Belly up to the soda fountain and enjoy a Pepsi, or browse around for Pepsi souvenirs.

U.S.S. *North Carolina*

Wilmington

★ **Battleship North Carolina Memorial:** Head down to the dock on the Cape Fear River and climb aboard the U.S.S. *North Carolina* for a tour. This battleship played a major role in the Pacific Ocean during World War II.

★ **The Cotton Exchange:** This strip of buildings from the early 1900s recalls the time when Wilmington was one of the world's major cotton-shipping ports. Now the buildings house more than 30 shops and restaurants.

★ **Ghost Walk of Old Wilmington:** Join ghost hunters and actors on a spooky tour of the winding alley-ways of Old Wilmington.

North Carolina has some odd place-names. It has towns named Frying Pan Landing, Gum Neck, Sandy Mush, Lizard Lick, and Whynot!

THE PIEDMONT

THINGS TO DO: Wander through Civil War battlefields, tour the state capitol, and discover the wonders of science, nature, and history through a variety of museums.

Bailey

★ **Country Doctor Museum:** Here you can see medical equipment that country doctors used more than a century ago and learn all about the odd techniques and tonics they used to cure the sick. This museum will make you glad you didn't live in the 1800s!

High Point

★ **World's Largest Chest of Drawers:** It's 40 feet (12 m) high! It was built to call attention to High Point as the Furniture Capital of the World. Two 6-foot (1.8 m) socks dangle from one of the drawers. They stand for the city's hosiery industry.

World's Largest Chest of Drawers

Raleigh

★ **State Legislative Building:** This modern building stands just a block north of the capitol. When the legislature is in session, you can sit in the gallery and watch state lawmakers at work.

★ **North Carolina Museum of History:** See the state's history come alive as you explore a dugout canoe, flags, Civil War photos, a model of the Wright brothers' plane, and much more. The museum also houses the North Carolina Sports Hall of Fame.

★ **North Carolina Museum of Natural Sciences:** Meet Willo, the world's only dinosaur with a fossilized heart. You'll also meet an *Acrocanthosaurus* dinosaur nicknamed the "Terror of the South" because of its long, pointy spines.

Dinosaur exhibit at the North Carolina Museum of Natural Sciences

★ **State Capitol:** Tour this elegant 1840 building that once housed all three branches of state government. Now it's partly a government building and partly a museum.

★ **African American Cultural Complex:** Housed in several cottages along a nature trail, this museum exhibits artifacts, documents, and displays of outstanding contributions made by African Americans.

Durham

★ **North Carolina Museum of Life and Science:** Use interactive exhibits to explore aerospace, weather, geology, and much more. At the outdoor woodland and wetland site, you can observe animals in their natural habitats.

★ **Duke Homestead and Tobacco Museum:** See where the Duke family began their tobacco empire. You'll tour the original Duke home and farm buildings, as well as a modern museum with interactive multimedia exhibits.

★ **Stagville Center:** This former tobacco plantation includes a barn and four original cabins where enslaved people lived. The center also offers programs on African American history and slave culture.

Lions at the North Carolina Zoological Park

Asheboro

★ **North Carolina Zoological Park:**
See more than 700 animals and
30,000 plants. The park covers
1,448 acres (586 ha), making it one
of the largest zoos in the world.

Chapel Hill

★ **Morehead Planetarium and
Science Center:** Watch a star show
in the gigantic dome theater, join
a sky-watching session under the
starry night sky, and learn about
chemistry and physics through live
demonstrations.

Burlington

★ **Alamance Battleground:** This is
where 2,000 frontiersmen called
the Regulators rebelled against
wealthy plantation owners in 1771.
On the grounds is a log home
called the Allen House. Built in
1780, it's the type of house the
frontier people lived in.

Four Oaks

★ **Bentonville Battlefield:** On
this site, Union forces defeated
Confederate troops in March 1865.
This was the largest land battle of
the Civil War to take place in North
Carolina, with 80,000 soldiers
involved.

Greensboro

★ **International Civil Rights Center
and Museum:** This museum of
African American history is housed
in the old Woolworth's building
where four African American
college students held the first civil
rights sit-in in 1960.

★ **Guilford Courthouse National
Military Park:** This park honors
the Revolutionary War battle of
1781. Stop by the visitors' center
to watch the animated battle map,
then walk the trails to see the
battle site itself, with monuments
and informational exhibits.

Reenactment of the Battle of Guilford Courthouse

Winston-Salem

★ **SciWorks:** Watch the solar system unfold in the planetarium, come face-to-face with river otters in the environmental park, and try out hundreds of hands-on science exhibits.

Charlotte

★ **Levine Museum of the New South:** Learn all about modern southern history, from sharecropping to NASCAR racing. Cotton Fields to Skyscrapers, a huge exhibit, illustrates the profound changes in the South since the Civil War.

SEE IT HERE!

OLD SALEM

Get a whiff of colonial life in this settlement founded by members of the Moravian Church in 1766. Your nose will lead you to Winkler Bakery. It's still baking bread, cakes, and pastries in a wood-burning oven, just as it has since 1807. Stroll the streets and see costumed tradespeople bustle about in every shop. They demonstrate making furniture, tools, and foods. You'll even meet the schoolmaster of the boys' school. At the Old Salem Toy Museum, you'll see more than 1,200 toys from around the world, through 1,700 years of history. And don't miss the Old Salem Children's Museum. It's a great place to learn about colonial life by experimenting and building things.

★ **Discovery Place:** Wander through a rain forest, peer inside a huge eyeball, and sample some liquid-nitrogen ice cream at this hands-on science museum.

★ **Mint Museum of Art:** North Carolina's first art museum, this institution is in the building that once housed the first branch of the U.S. Mint. It features a diverse collection that includes American art, European ceramics, and historic costumes.

★ **Afro-American Cultural Center:** This museum in an old church building houses an art collection highlighting African American history and culture. The outdoor amphitheater features films and live presentations of jazz, poetry, and other performing arts.

Carvings at the Afro-American Cultural Center

THE MOUNTAINS

THINGS TO DO: Climb a mountain peak, sway on a swinging bridge, ride a train through mountain tunnels and valleys, see corn ground into cornmeal, or wander through a Cherokee village.

Linville

★ **Grandfather Mountain:** This mountain looks like the face of an old man sleeping. Walk across the mountain's Mile High Swinging Bridge for a spectacular view across the Blue Ridge Mountains. Back on solid ground, you can view wildlife habitats for black bears, cougars, and other wild animals.

SEE IT HERE!

BLUE RIDGE PARKWAY

The scenic Blue Ridge Parkway runs along the peaks of the Blue Ridge Mountains. It stretches from Virginia through northwestern North Carolina for 469 miles (755 km), winding through forests, mountain meadows, and wetlands. Along the parkway, you can hike or bike along hundreds of trails through the woods to watch wildlife, go fishing, look out across the mountains, take photos, or have a picnic.

Biltmore Estate

Asheville

★ **Biltmore Estate:** This is the largest home in the United States. Millionaire George W. Vanderbilt built it in the early 1900s. Tour the massive, elegant mansion, then stroll around the estate's grounds.

Burnsville

★ **Mount Mitchell State Park:** Enjoy camping, picnicking, hiking, and wildlife watching in this forested park. The centerpiece is Mount Mitchell, North Carolina's highest peak.

Chimney Rock

★ **Chimney Rock Park:** The Chimney is an unusual rock formation towering high above the surrounding mountains. Hike the trails, and you'll come upon 404-foot (123 m) Hickory Nut Falls and the Needle's Eye, a narrow crevice in the rocks.

Cherokee

★ *Unto These Hills* **Outdoor Drama:** Learn what it means to be Cherokee as you follow the events in this dramatic play. It traces the history of the region's Cherokee people from 1540 until their forced march west in the late 1830s on the Trail of Tears.

Great Smoky Mountains National Park

★ **Mountain Farm Museum and Mingus Mill:** Here you can explore a log farmhouse, barn, apple house, and working blacksmith shop to see how families lived 100 years ago. Take some cornmeal home from the mill and make a batch of delicious muffins!

★ **Clingmans Dome:** This peak on the Tennessee–North Carolina border is the highest point in Great Smoky Mountains National Park. On a clear day, you can see into seven states from the observation tower.

The observation tower at Clingmans Dome

★ **Museum of the Cherokee Indian:** Your guide at this museum is a **holographic** medicine man who takes you on a journey through time. On your journey, you learn about the legends, traditions, and lifeways sacred to Cherokees.

WORD TO KNOW

holographic *appearing as a computer-generated image*

★ **Oconaluftee Indian Village:** This is a re-created Native American village of the 1750s. As your Cherokee guide takes you through the village, you'll hear ancient stories and watch Cherokee artisans at work.

Bryson City

★ **Great Smoky Mountains Railroad:** Hop aboard! This train takes you over mountains, through mountain tunnels, into deep river gorges, and across fertile valleys.

★ **Nantahala Gorge:** Sunlight only reaches the bottom of the gorge around midday. That's why Cherokees named it *Nantahala*, meaning "land of the noonday sun." It is in Nantahala National Forest.

SCIENCE, TECHNOLOGY, & MATH PROJECTS

Make weather maps, graph population statistics, and research endangered species that live in the state.

120

PRIMARY VS. SECONDARY SOURCES

121

So what are primary and secondary sources? And what's the diff? This section explains all that and where you can find them.

133

BIOGRAPHICAL DICTIONARY

This at-a-glance guide highlights some of the state's most important and influential people. Visit this section and read about their contributions to the state, the country, and the world.

RESOURCES

Books, Web sites, DVDs, and more. Take a look at these additional sources for information about the state.

137

WRITING PROJECTS

★ ★ ★

Write a Memoir, Journal, or Editorial for Your School Newspaper!

Picture Yourself . . .

★ Living in a Cherokee village, playing stickball, hunting for food, and engaging in ritual dance around the fire or near the great river.

   SEE: Chapter Two, pages 30–33.

★ Working on a colonial farm. What would your responsibilities be? What kinds of adventures could you experience on the colonial frontier?

   SEE: Chapter Three, pages 34–45.

★ Being forced from your homeland, leaving everything behind, and walking to a faraway place along the Trail of Tears.

   SEE: Chapter Four, pages 51–53.

Create an Election Brochure or Web Site!

Run for office! Throughout this book, you've read about some of the issues that concern North Carolina today. As a candidate for governor of North Carolina, create a campaign brochure or Web site.

★ Explain how you meet the qualifications to be governor of North Carolina.

★ Talk about the three or four major issues you'll focus on if you're elected.

★ Remember, you'll be responsible for North Carolina's budget. How would you spend the taxpayers' money?

   SEE: Chapter Seven, pages 86–95.

   GO TO: North Carolina's government Web site at www.nc.gov. You may also want to read some local newspapers. Try these:

   Charlotte Observer at www.charlotte.com

   News & Observer (Raleigh) at www.newsobserver.com

   Winston-Salem Journal at www.journalnow.com

Create an interview script with a person from North Carolina!

★ Research various North Carolinians, such as Mia Hamm, William Tryon, Joseph McNeil, Betsy Byars, Levi Coffin, and Sequoyah.

★ Based on your research, pick one person you would most like to interview.

★ Write a script of the interview. What questions would you ask? How would this person answer? Create a question-and-answer format. You may want to supplement this writing project with a voice-recording dramatization of the interview.

   SEE: Chapters Five, Six, and Seven, pages 62–95, and the Biographical Dictionary, pages 133–136.

   GO TO: www.secstate.state.nc.us/kidspg/famous.htm

ART PROJECTS

★ ★ ★

Create a PowerPoint Presentation or Visitors' Guide

Welcome to North Carolina!

North Carolina is a great place to visit and to live! From its natural beauty to its bustling cities and historical sites, there's plenty to see and do. In your PowerPoint presentation or brochure, highlight 10 to 15 of North Carolina's fascinating landmarks. Be sure to include:

★ a map of the state showing where these sites are located

★ photos, illustrations, Web links, natural history facts, geographic stats, climate and weather, plants and wildlife, and recent discoveries

SEE: Chapter Nine, pages 106–115, and Fast Facts, pages 126–127.

GO TO: The official tourism Web site for North Carolina at www.visitnc.com. Download and print maps, photos, and vacation ideas for tourists.

Illustrate the Lyrics to the North Carolina State Song

("The Old North State")

Use markers, paints, photos, collages, colored pencils, or computer graphics to illustrate the lyrics to "The Old North State." Turn your illustrations into a picture book, or scan them into PowerPoint and add music.

SEE: The lyrics to "The Old North State" on page 128.

GO TO: The North Carolina state government Web site at www.nc.gov to find out more about the origin of the state song.

State Quarter Project

From 1999 to 2008, the U.S. Mint introduced new quarters commemorating each of the 50 states in the order that they were admitted to the Union. Each state's quarter features a unique design on its back, or reverse.

★ Go to www.usmint.gov/kids and find out what's featured on the back of the North Carolina quarter.

★ Research the significance of the image. Who designed the quarter? Who chose the final design?

★ Design your own North Carolina quarter. What images would you choose for the reverse?

★ Make a poster showing the North Carolina quarter and label each image.

SCIENCE, TECHNOLOGY, & MATH PROJECTS

★ ★ ★

Graph Population Statistics!

★ Compare population statistics (such as ethnic background, birth, death, and literacy rates) in North Carolina counties or major cities.

★ In your graph or chart, look at population density and write sentences describing what the population statistics show; graph one set of population statistics and write a paragraph explaining what the graphs reveal.

SEE: Chapter Six, pages 74–77.

GO TO: Check out the official Web site for the U.S. Census Bureau at www.census.gov and at http://quickfacts.census.gov/qfd/states/37000.html, to find out more about population statistics, how they work, and what the statistics are for North Carolina.

Create a Weather Map of North Carolina!

Use your knowledge of North Carolina's geography to research and identify conditions that result in specific weather events. What is it about the geography of North Carolina that makes it vulnerable to things such as tornadoes and hurricanes? Create a weather map or poster that shows the weather patterns over the state. To accompany your map, explain the technology used to measure weather phenomena and provide data.

SEE: Chapter One, pages 8–23.

GO TO: Visit the National Oceanic and Atmospheric Administration's National Weather Service Web site at www.weather.gov for weather maps and forecasts for North Carolina.

Eastern cougar

Track Endangered Species

Using your knowledge of North Carolina's wildlife, research what animals and plants are endangered or threatened.

★ Find out what the state is doing to protect these species.

★ Chart known populations of the animals and plants, and report on changes in certain geographic areas.

SEE: Chapter One, pages 18–23.

GO TO: Web sites such as www.fws.gov/nc-es/es/es.html for lists of endangered species in North Carolina

PRIMARY VS. SECONDARY SOURCES

★ ★ ★

What's the Diff?

Your teacher may require at least one or two primary sources and one or two secondary sources for your assignment. So, what's the difference between the two?

★ **Primary sources are original.** You are reading the actual words of someone's diary, journal, letter, autobiography, or interview. Primary sources can also be photographs, maps, prints, cartoons, news/film footage, posters, first-person newspaper articles, drawings, musical scores, and recordings. By the way, when you conduct a survey, interview someone, shoot a video, or take photographs to include in a project, you are creating primary sources!

★ **Secondary sources are what you find in encyclopedias, textbooks, articles, biographies, and almanacs.** These are written by a person or group of people who tell about something that happened to someone else. Secondary sources also recount what another person said or did. This book is an example of a secondary source.

Now that you know what primary sources are—where can you find them?

★ **Your school or local library:** Check the library catalog for collections of original writings, government documents, musical scores, and so on. Some of this material may be stored on microfilm. The Library of Congress Web site (www.loc.gov) is an excellent online resource for primary source materials.

★ **Historical societies:** These organizations keep historical documents, photographs, and other materials. Staff members can help you find what you are looking for. History museums are also great places to see primary sources firsthand.

★ **The Internet:** There are lots of sites that have primary sources you can download and use in a project or assignment.

TIMELINE

★ ★ ★

| U.S. Events | 1500 | North Carolina Events |

1540
Europeans and North Carolina's Native Americans first make contact.

1565
Spanish admiral Pedro Menéndez de Avilés founds St. Augustine, Florida, the oldest continuously occupied European settlement in the continental United States.

1585
Sir Walter Raleigh sends settlers to establish the first English colony on Roanoke Island. A second colony is founded in 1587, but it disappears in 1590.

1600

1607
The first permanent English settlement in North America is established at Jamestown.

Sir Walter Raleigh

1620
Pilgrims found Plymouth Colony, the second permanent English settlement.

1629
King Charles I of England grants the Province of Carolana to Sir Robert Heath.

c. 1653
North Carolina's first permanent settlers come from Virginia to settle in the Albemarle region.

1663
King Charles II grants the Carolina colony to eight lords, who divide it into three counties.

1700

1711–15
The Tuscarora people fight white settlers in the Tuscarora War.

1729
North Carolina is sold back to England, and royal governors rule the region.

1754–63
England and France fight over North American colonial lands in the French and Indian War. By the end of the war, France cedes all of its land west of the Mississippi to Spain and its Canadian territories to England.

U.S. Events

North Carolina Events

1774
North Carolina sends delegates to the First Continental Congress in Philadelphia, Pennsylvania.

1776
Thirteen American colonies declare their independence from Great Britain.

1776
The Battle of Moore's Creek Bridge is North Carolina's first battle in the Revolutionary War; North Carolina becomes the first state to vote for independence.

1781
British troops withdraw from North Carolina, later surrendering in Virginia.

1787
The U.S. Constitution is written.

1800

1789
North Carolina becomes the 12th state of the United States of America.

1803
The Louisiana Purchase almost doubles the size of the United States.

1830
The Indian Removal Act forces eastern Native American groups to relocate west of the Mississippi River.

1838
In what is called the Trail of Tears, the U.S. government forces Cherokees to move to Oklahoma.

1861–65
The American Civil War is fought between the Northern Union and the Southern Confederacy; it ends with the surrender of the Confederate army, led by General Robert E. Lee.

1861
North Carolina secedes from the Union shortly after the Civil War begins.

1863
President Abraham Lincoln frees all slaves in the Southern Confederacy with the Emancipation Proclamation.

1868
North Carolina rejoins the Union.

1900

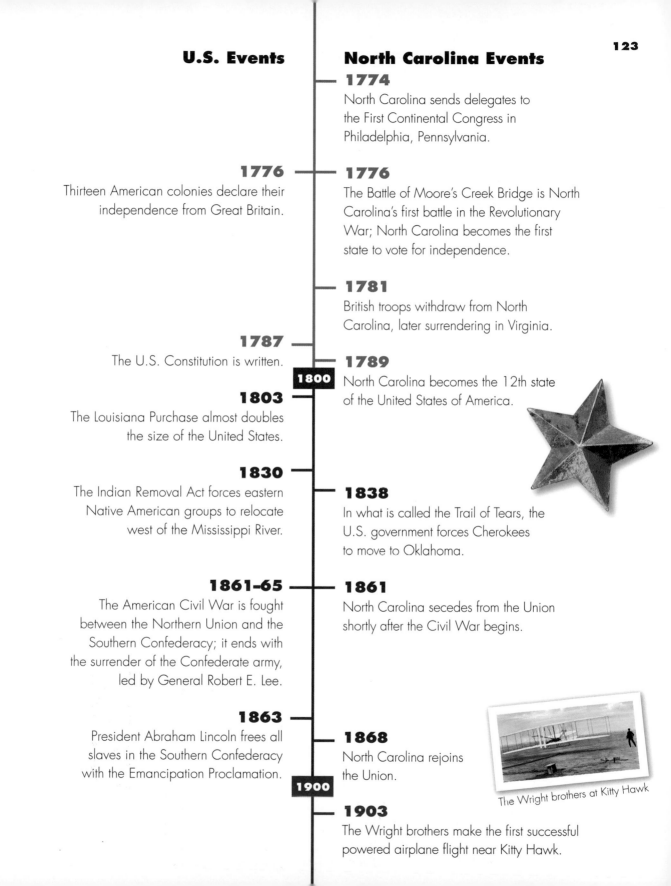

The Wright brothers at Kitty Hawk

1903
The Wright brothers make the first successful powered airplane flight near Kitty Hawk.

U.S. Events

North Carolina Events

1915
As more people own automobiles, North Carolina sets up a highway commission.

1917–18
The United States engages in World War I.

1929
The stock market crashes, plunging the United States more deeply into the Great Depression.

1941–45
The United States engages in World War II.

Medical researchers at Duke University

1951–53
The United States engages in the Korean War.

1959
Research Triangle Park opens, beginning an era of high-tech growth.

1960
Four black students in Greensboro hold the nation's first sit-in to protest racial segregation.

1964–73
The United States engages in the Vietnam War.

1972
Governor James Holshouser Jr. and U.S. senator Jesse Helms become the first Republicans from North Carolina elected to those offices since the 1890s.

1980s
The textile and furniture industries begin to decline.

1991
The United States and other nations engage in the brief Persian Gulf War against Iraq.

1999
Hurricane Floyd causes flooding that devastates eastern North Carolina.

2000

2001
Terrorists hijack four U.S. aircraft and crash them into the World Trade Center in New York City, the Pentagon in Arlington, Virginia, and a Pennsylvania field, killing thousands.

2003
The United States and coalition forces invade Iraq.

2007
The business magazine *Forbes* names five North Carolina cities as among the best places to do business or start a career.

GLOSSARY

★ ★ ★

abolitionists people who work to end slavery

alliance an association between groups that benefits all the members

artifacts objects remaining from a particular period of time

Bill of Rights the first ten amendments to the Constitution, which list the fundamental rights guaranteed to Americans

biotechnology the manipulation of living organisms for developments in the areas of food production, waste disposal, mining, and medicine

blowguns weapons that consist of tubes through which darts are blown

civil rights basic human rights that all citizens in a society are entitled to, such as the right to vote

constitution a written document that contains all the governing principles of a state or country

dialect a version of a language

discrimination unequal treatment based on race, gender, religion, or other factors

emissions substances released into the air

fugitive a person who tries to flee or escape

holographic appearing as a computer-generated image

impeached charged with official misconduct while in office

integrate to bring together all members of society

missionary related to trying to convert others to a religion

palisades fences of logs set vertically into the ground close to each other to create a protected village

Parliament the legislature in Great Britain

pharmaceutical relating to the manufacture and sale of drugs used in medicine

precipitation all water that falls to the earth, including rain, sleet, hail, snow, dew, fog, or mist

segregated separated from others, according to race, class, ethnic group, religion, or other factors

sit-ins acts of protest that involve sitting in seats or on the floor of an establishment and refusing to leave

sounds long, wide inlets of the ocean along a coast

tidewaters low coastal land that is affected by tides

FAST FACTS

★ ★ ★

State Symbols

Statehood date	November 21, 1789, the 12th state
Origin of state name	Named for King Charles I in a land grant given to Sir Robert Heath
State capital	Raleigh
State nickname	Tar Heel State, Old North State
State motto	*Esse quam videri* (To be, rather than to seem)
State bird	Cardinal
State flower	Flowering dogwood
State fish	Channel bass
State gem	Emerald
State song	"The Old North State"
State tree	Longleaf Pine
State fair	Raleigh (mid-October)

State seal

Geography

Total area; rank	53,819 square miles (139,391 sq km); 28th
Land area; rank	48,711 square miles (126,161 sq km); 29th
Water area; rank	5,108 square miles (13,230 sq km); 10th
Inland water; rank	3,960 square miles (10,256 sq km); 6th
Territorial water; rank	1,148 square miles (2,973 sq km); 10th
Geographic center	Chatham County, 10 miles (16 km) northwest of Sanford
Latitude	34° N to 36°21' N
Longitude	75°30' W to 84°15' W
Highest point	Mount Mitchell, 6,684 feet (2,037 m), in Yancey
Lowest point	Sea level along the Atlantic coast
Largest city	Charlotte
Number of counties	100
Longest river	Cape Fear River, 200 miles (322 km)

Population

Population; rank (2006 estimate)	8,856,505; 10th
Density (2006 estimate):	182 persons per square mile (70 per sq km)
Population distribution (2000 census):	60% urban, 40% rural
Ethnic distribution (2005 estimate)	White persons: 74.1%*
	Black persons: 21.8%*
	Asian persons: 1.8%*
	American Indian and Alaska Native persons: 1.3%*
	Native Hawaiian and Other Pacific Islanders: 0.1%*
	Persons reporting two or more races: 1.0%
	Persons of Hispanic or Latino origin: 6.4%†
	White persons not Hispanic: 68.3%

Includes persons reporting only one race.
† Hispanics may be of any race, so they are also included in applicable race categories.

Weather

Record high temperature	110°F (43°C) at Fayetteville on August 21, 1983
Record low temperature	−34°F (−37°C) at Mount Mitchell on January 21, 1985
Average July temperature	79°F (26°C)
Average January temperature	40°F (4°C)
Average annual precipitation	43 inches (109 cm)

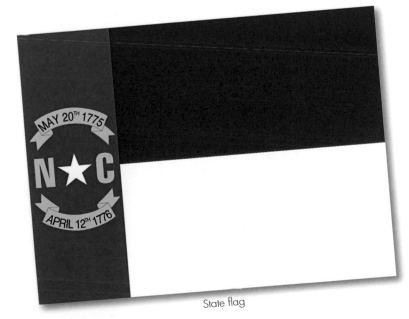

State flag

STATE SONG

★　★　★

"The Old North State"

The General Assembly of 1927 adopted the song "The Old North State" as the official song of North Carolina. It is based on a traditional tune arranged by Mrs. E. E. Randolph, with words by William Gaston.

Carolina! Carolina
Heaven's blessings attend her,
While we live, we will cherish, protect and defend her.
Tho' the scorner may sneer at and witlings defame her,
Still our hearts swell with gladness whenever we name her.

Hurrah! Hurrah!
The Old North State forever.
Hurrah! Hurrah!
The good Old North State.

Tho' she envies not others, their merited glory,
Say whose name stands foremost, in liberty's story.
Tho' too true to herself e'er to crouch to oppression,
Who can yield to just rule a more loyal submission.

Hurrah! Hurrah!
The Old North State forever.
Hurrah! Hurrah!
The good Old North State.

Then let all those who love us,
Love the land that we live in,
As happy a region as on this side of heaven,
Where plenty and peace, love and joy smile before us,
Raise aloud, raise together the heart-thrilling chorus.

Hurrah! Hurrah!
The Old North State forever.
Hurrah! Hurrah!
The good Old North State.

NATURAL AREAS AND HISTORIC SITES

National Park
The state's only national park is the *Great Smoky Mountains National Park*, which stretches across the border between North Carolina and Tennessee.

National Memorial
North Carolina is home to the *Wright Brothers National Memorial*, which honors the efforts of the Wright brothers, who created the world's first powered airplane.

National Seashores
The state features two national seashores: *Cape Hatteras National Seashore*, which spans more than 70 miles (110 km) and includes many shipwrecks, lighthouses, and lifeguard stations, and *Cape Lookout National Seashore.*

National Military Park and National Battlefield
North Carolina has one national military park and one national battlefield. *Guilford Courthouse National Military Park* is the site of a fierce Revolutionary War battle. *Moores Creek National Battlefield* honors those involved in the 1776 battle that ended British control in North Carolina.

Parkway
The state's *Blue Ridge Parkway* is a 469-mile (755 km) drive filled with historical and cultural sites.

National Scenic Trail and National Historic Trails
Part of the 2,174-mile-long (3,499 km) *Appalachian National Scenic Trail* passes through North Carolina. Two national historic trails cross North Carolina, the *Overmountain Victory National Historic Trail* and the *Trail of Tears National Historic Trail.*

National Historic Sites
The state features two national historic sites: *Carl Sandburg Home National Historic Site* which honors Sandburg, a prominent writer and poet of the 20th century, and the *Fort Raleigh National Historic Site.*

National Forests
Pisgah, Nantahala, Uwharrie, and Croatan national forests cover more than 1.2 million acres (486,000 ha).

State Parks and Forests
North Carolina's state park system features 34 state parks and recreation areas, including *Carolina Beach State Park*, *Gorges State Park*, *Hanging Rock State Park*, and the *Fort Macon State Park*. Six of the state forests are designated as Education State Forests, which are designed to teach the public—especially schoolchildren—about the forest environment.

SPORTS TEAMS

NCAA Teams (Division I)

Appalachian State University *Mountaineers*
Campbell University *Camels*
Davidson College *Wildcats*
Duke University *Blue Devils*
East Carolina University *Pirates*
Elon University *Phoenixes*
Gardner-Webb University *Bulldogs*
High Point University *Panthers*
North Carolina A&T State University *Aggies*

North Carolina State University *Wolfpack*
University of North Carolina–Asheville *Bulldogs*
University of North Carolina–Chapel Hill *Tar Heels*
University of North Carolina–Charlotte *49ers*
University of North Carolina–Greensboro *Spartans*
University of North Carolina–Wilmington *Seahawks*
Wake Forest University *Demon Deacons*
Western Carolina University *Catamounts*

PROFESSIONAL SPORTS TEAMS

National Basketball Association
Charlotte *Bobcats*

National Football League
Carolina *Panthers*

National Hockey League
Carolina *Hurricanes*

Women's National Basketball Association
Charlotte *Sting*

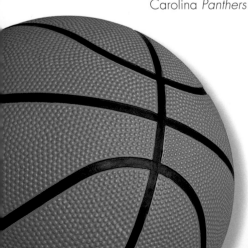

CULTURAL INSTITUTIONS

★　★　★

Libraries

The *University of North Carolina–Chapel Hill* and *Duke University Library* have the largest library collections in the state.

The *North Carolina State Library* (Raleigh) and the *State Department of Archives and History* (Raleigh) both hold significant collections on state history.

Museums

The *Greensboro Historical Museum* and the *North Carolina Museum of History* (Raleigh) have extensive collections relating to the state's history.

The *North Carolina Aquariums* (Raleigh, Pine Knoll Shores, and Fort Fisher) help promote an understanding and appreciation of the diverse natural and cultural resources associated with North Carolina's oceans, estuaries, rivers, streams, and other aquatic environments.

The *North Carolina Museum of Art* (Raleigh) is the only art museum in the United States that started with state funding.

The *North Carolina Museum of Natural Sciences* (Raleigh) looks at the natural world through the lens of North Carolina's diverse geography, geology, plants, and animals.

The *North Carolina Transportation Museum* (Spencer) features an authentic train depot, antique automobiles, and a 37-bay roundhouse that includes 25 locomotives, dozens of rail cars, and other exhibit areas.

The *North Carolina Maritime Museum* (Beaufort) features programs and exhibits that interpret the state's cultural maritime history and offer a larger national perspective on coastal environment and barrier island ecology.

William Hayes Ackland Memorial Art Center (Chapel Hill) and the *Weatherspoon Art Gallery* (Greensboro) are important museums within the University of North Carolina system.

Performing Arts

North Carolina has one major opera company, three major symphony orchestras, and two major dance companies.

Universities and Colleges

In 2006, North Carolina had 74 public and 55 private institutions of higher learning.

★ ★ ANNUAL EVENTS

January–March

Field Trials in Pinehurst (January)

Camellia Show in Wilmington (February)

Horse Trials in Tryon (March)

Moravian Easter Service in Old Salem (March or April)

April–June

Azalea Festival in Wilmington (April)

Shad Festival in Grifton (April)

Stoneybrook Steeplechase in Southern Pines (April)

Festival of Flowers at Biltmore Estate in Asheville (April–May)

Annual Emerald Isle Beach Music Festival in Emerald Isle (May)

Ole Time Fiddler's and Bluegrass Festival in Union Grove (May)

National Hollerin' Contest in Spivey's Corner near Fayetteville (June)

Rhododendron Festival in the Bakersville area (June)

Singing on the Mountain at Grandfather Mountain near Linville (June)

Summer Festival of Music in Brevard (June–August)

July–September

Bele Chere Festival in Asheville (July)

Highland Games and Gathering of Scottish Clans at Grandfather Mountain (July)

Western North Carolina Wagon Train in Brevard (July)

Annual Mount Mitchell Crafts Fair in Burnsville (August)

Mountain Dance and Folk Festival in Asheville (August)

North Carolina Apple Festival in Hendersonville (Labor Day weekend)

Benson Mule Days in Benson (September)

State Championship Horse Show in Raleigh (September)

October–December

State Fair in Raleigh (October)

Surf Fishing Tournament in Nags Head (October)

Anniversary of First Powered Airplane Flight in Kill Devil Hills (December)

Christmas at Biltmore in Asheville (December)

Christmas at the Homestead in Boone (December)

Candlelight Christmas Tour of Historic Oakwood in Raleigh (December)

Penelope Barker See page 42.

David Brinkley (1920–2003) was a TV newscaster. He hosted ABC's *This Week with David Brinkley* (1981–1996) and coanchored NBC's *Huntley-Brinkley Report* (1956–1970). He was born in Wilmington.

Betsy Byars See page 80.

Levi Coffin See page 51.

John Coltrane (1926–1967) was a saxophonist and composer, considered one of the greatest jazz musicians of all time. Born in Hamlet, he influenced many musicians of his day and later.

Howard Cosell (1918–1995) was a sportscaster who starred for many years on ABC-TV's *Monday Night Football*. He was also the commentator for many of legendary boxer Muhammad Ali's fights. Cosell was born in Winston-Salem.

Virginia Dare (1587–1597?) was the first child born in North America to English parents. She was born on Roanoke Island in the so-called Lost Colony of Roanoke.

Roberta Flack

Chris Daughtry (1979–) placed fourth in the 2006 *American Idol* competition and went on to have a number-one-selling CD with his band, Daughtry. He was born in Roanoke Rapids.

Thomas Day (c. 1801–1861) was a furniture maker who started his business in Milton in the 1820s. His pieces are still highly valued today.

Sarah Dessen (1970–) is an author of young adult novels. Her many popular books include *That Summer*, *Someone Like You*, *The Truth About Forever*, *This Lullaby*, and *Just Listen*. She grew up in Chapel Hill.

Chris Daughtry

Elizabeth Hanford Dole See page 71.

Dale Earnhardt Sr. (1951–2001) was one of the greatest race-car drivers in NASCAR history. He won seven Winston Cup championships. Born in Kannapolis, he was killed in Florida's Daytona 500 race.

John Edwards See page 91.

Roberta Flack (1939–) is a jazz and soul singer. Her hits include "The First Time Ever I Saw Your Face" and "Killing Me Softly with His Song." She was born in Asheville.

Henry Frye See page 92.

Ava Gardner (1922–1990) was an actor whose many films include *The Killers*, *The Night of the Iguana*, and *Mogambo*, for which she received an Academy Award nomination. She was born in Brogden and was buried in Smithfield, where the Ava Gardner Museum is located.

134

Andy Griffith (1926–) is an actor who played the laid-back sheriff of Mayberry in *The Andy Griffith Show* and the country lawyer Ben Matlock in *Matlock*. He was born in Mount Airy.

Michael C. Hall (1971–) is an actor who has appeared in the cable TV series *Six Feet Under* and *Dexter*. He was born in Raleigh.

Mia Hamm See page 84.

O. Henry is the pen name of **William Sydney Porter (1862–1910)**, whose short stories include "The Ransom of Red Chief" and "The Gift of the Magi." He was born on Polecat Creek and raised in Greensboro.

Andrew Jackson (1767–1845) See page 91.

Andrew Johnson (1808–1875) See page 91.

Michael Jordan See page 83.

Charles Kuralt (1934–1997) was a TV journalist. He presented "On the Road" segments on the *CBS Evening News* before hosting *CBS News Sunday Morning* for 15 years. He was born in Wilmington.

Charles Kuralt

Kay Kyser (1905–1985) was a popular bandleader during the big-band era of the 1940s. He and his band appeared in many 1940s movies, too. He was born James Kern Kyser in Rocky Mount.

Sugar Ray Leonard (1956–) won the gold medal for boxing at the 1976 Olympics and won five world boxing titles. He was born in Wilmington as Ray Charles Leonard.

Joseph McNeil See page 68.

Ronnie Milsap (1943–) is a country music superstar whose style eventually crossed over into country pop. He recorded 40 number-one country hits. He was born in Robbinsville.

Elisha Mitchell See page 11.

Thelonious Monk (1917–1982) was a jazz pianist, composer, and founder of the bebop style of jazz. "'Round Midnight" is one of his classic works. He was born in Rocky Mount.

Shelia P. Moses See page 81.

Sugar Ray Leonard

Frankie Muniz (1985–) is an actor who starred in the TV series *Malcolm in the Middle* and won an Emmy Award for his role in 2001. Born in New Jersey, he grew up in Knightsbridge.

Edward R. Murrow (1908–1965) was a pioneering TV news journalist known around the world for his exceptional reporting. His trademark was to end his broadcasts with "Good night, and good luck." He was born near Polecat Creek in Guilford County.

Gaylord Perry (1938–) was a pitcher for the San Francisco Giants, the New York Yankees, the Atlanta Braves, and other teams. He totaled 314 wins and 3,534 strikeouts. He was born in Williamston.

Richard Petty See page 85.

James K. Polk (1795–1849) See page 91.

William Sydney Porter. See O. Henry.

Jaime Pressly (1977–) is a model and actor who plays Joy Turner in the TV comedy *My Name Is Earl*. She was born in Kinston.

Emily Procter (1968–) is a TV actor who has appeared on *The West Wing* and *CSI: Miami*. She was born in Raleigh.

Emily Procter

Charlie Rose (1942–) is a journalist and interviewer. He hosts an interview and talk show on public television. He was born in Henderson.

Earl Scruggs (1924–) is a banjo player whose finger-picking style became the hallmark of bluegrass music. He and guitarist Lester Flatt provided the music for the TV show *The Beverly Hillbillies* and the movie *Bonnie and Clyde*. Scruggs was born in Madison.

Amy Sedaris (1961–) is a comic actor who appeared in the TV comedy series *Strangers with Candy*. She has also performed in several movies. Born in New York, she grew up in Raleigh.

David Sedaris (1956–) is a comic author, playwright, and frequent commentator on National Public Radio. Among his books are *Me Talk Pretty One Day* and *The Santaland Diaries*. Born in New York, he was raised in Raleigh.

Sequoyah See page 52.

Gaylord Perry

Nina Simone (1933–2003) was a jazz, blues, and soul singer. In the 1960s, she often used her songs and concerts to convey messages about civil rights. She was born in Tryon as Eunice Kathleen Waymon.

James Taylor (1948–) is a singer and songwriter. *Carolina in My Mind*, *Fire and Rain*, and *Sweet Baby James* brought him fame in the 1970s. Born in Massachusetts, he grew up in Chapel Hill.

Theodore Taylor (1921–2006) wrote more than 50 books for young adults. His book *The Cay* concerns a boy who escaped from a sinking ship in 1942. Born in Statesville, he grew up in Craddock.

Randy Travis (1959–) is a country singer and songwriter with more than a dozen number-one country hit songs. He was born in Marshville.

William Tryon See page 41.

Reginald VelJohnson

Reginald VelJohnson (1968–) is a TV and movie actor who has appeared in the TV comedy *Family Matters* and in many movies. He was born in Raleigh.

David Walker See page 50.

Mary Elizabeth Winstead (1984–) is a movie actor whose credits include *Sky High*, *Bobby*, *Final Destination 3*, *Live Free or Die Hard*, and *Death Proof*. She was born in Rocky Mount.

Thomas Wolfe (1900–1938) wrote the classic novels *Look Homeward, Angel* and *You Can't Go Home Again*. He often used scenes from his Asheville hometown in his books.

Evan Rachel Wood (1987–) is an actor whose movie credits include *Thirteen* and *Pretty Persuasion*. She received a Golden Globe nomination for her role in *Thirteen*. She was born in Raleigh.

Kristi Yamaguchi (1971–) is a champion figure skater. She won world championships in 1991 and 1992 and the gold medal at the 1992 Olympics. Born in California, she later moved to Raleigh.

Kristi Yamaguchi

RESOURCES

BOOKS

Nonfiction

Cannavale, Matthew C. *Voices from Colonial America: North Carolina 1524–1776.* Washington, D.C.: National Geographic Children's Books, 2007.

Goldman, Phyllis. *Explore North Carolina's Economy, Communities, and Environment.* Greensboro, N.C.: Monkeyshines Publishers, 2001.

Margulies, Phillip. *A Primary Source History of the Colony of North Carolina.* New York: Rosen Central Primary Source, 2006.

Marsh, Carole. *North Carolina History!: Surprising Secrets About Our State's Founding Mothers, Fathers & Kids!* Peachtree City, Ga.: Gallopade International, 1996.

Taylor-Miller, Sandra. *Are We There Yet?: The Wright Brothers' National Memorial Park, Kill Devil Hills, North Carolina, Site of the First Heavier-Than-Air Machine-Powered Flight.* Boone, N.C.: Parkway Publishers, 2004.

Fiction

Alphin, Elaine Marie. *Ghost Soldier.* New York: Henry Holt, 2001.

Madden, Kerry. *Gentle's Holler.* New York: Puffin, 2007.

Moses, Shelia P. *The Legend of Buddy Bush.* New York: Margaret K. McElderry Books, 2004.

Wechter, Nell Wise. *Teach's Light: A Tale of Blackbeard the Pirate.* Chapel Hill: University of North Carolina Press, 1999.

White, Ruth. *Buttermilk Hill.* New York: Farrar, Straus and Giroux, 2004.

DVDs

At Work and At Play. Preservation North Carolina and Mark Spano Communications, in association with UNC-TV, 2000.

Discoveries . . . America: North Carolina. Bennett-Watt Entertainment, 2006.

Lighthouses of North Carolina's Outer Banks. CustomFlix, 2006.

On the Tracks of Progress. Preservation North Carolina and Mark Spano Communications, in association with UNC-TV, 1996.

A Passion for Place: A Fascinating Look at the Rich Heritage of North Carolina's Historic Buildings. Historic Preservation Foundation of North Carolina, Inc., and North Carolina State University, 1993.

WEB SITES AND ORGANIZATIONS

North Carolina Historic Sites
www.ah.dcr.state.nc.us/sections/ hs/sites.htm
To learn about North Carolina's 27 state historic sites.

North Carolina State Capitol
www.ah.dcr.state.nc.us/sections/hs/ capitol/default.htm
To learn all about the history of the capitol and the sights on the capitol tour.

North Carolina State Parks
www.ils.unc.edu/parkproject/visit/ ncmap.html
To read all about the sights and activities in each of North Carolina's state parks.

Official Web Site of the State of North Carolina
www.ncgov.com/
To learn about the state's government officials, agencies, and much more.

State of North Carolina Kids' Page
www.secretary.state.nc.us/kidspg/ ThePage.aspx
For tons of information on the state, including fun facts, legends, and ghost stories!

Visit North Carolina
www.visitnc.com/
To find out about places to go and things to do in the state.

INDEX

★ ★ ★

AUTHOR'S TIPS AND SOURCE NOTES

★ ★ ★

For information about North Carolina's earliest cultures, I found a wealth of information in *Intrigue of the Past: North Carolina's First Peoples* (www.rla. unc.edu/lessons/Menu/menu.htm). The state library's Web site includes a section called Historical Highlights of North Carolina (http://statelibrary. dcr.state.nc.us/NC/history/history.htm), which gives a detailed overview of the state's history from early times to the 20th century. Many good books shed light on North Carolina's history and culture, too. One is *The North Carolina Experience: An Interpretative and Documentary History,* edited by Lindley S. Butler and Alan D. Watson. It gives in-depth information on many subjects, such as Native American history, colonial life, civil rights, and the status of women. Another good history survey is *North Carolina: A History,* by William S. Powell. Milton Ready's *The Tar Heel State: A History of North Carolina* is jam-packed with information and is very readable.